THE
WISDOM
OF THE
UNIVERSE

by NEALE DONALD WALSCH

arranged and with photography by
SHERR ROBERTSON

A TarcherPerigee Book

THE WISDOM OF THE UNIVERSE

Essential Truths from
the Beloved *Conversations
with God* Trilogy

An imprint of Penguin Random House LLC
375 Hudson Street
New York, New York 10014

Selections from *Conversations with God* (Books 1, 2, and 3) published by
arrangement with Hampton Roads Press

TarcherPerigee with tp colophon is a registered trademark of
Penguin Random House LLC.

Most TarcherPerigee books are available at special quantity discounts for bulk
purchase for sales promotions, premiums, fund-raising, and educational needs.
Special books or book excerpts also can be created to fit specific needs. For
details, write: SpecialMarkets@penguinrandomhouse.com.

Library of Congress Cataloging-in-Publication Data

Names: Walsch, Neale Donald, author. | Robertson, Sherr, arranger,
photographer.
Title: The wisdom of the universe : essential truths from the beloved
Conversations with God trilogy / by Neale Donald Walsch ; arranged and with
photography by Sherr Robertson.
Description: First edition. | New York, NY : TarcherPerigee, 2017.
Identifiers: LCCN 2016018334 | ISBN 9780143109914 (pbk.)
Subjects: LCSH: Walsch, Neale Donald. Conversations with God. |
God—Miscellanea. | Spiritual life—Miscellanea. | Private revelations.
Classification: LCC BF1999 .W22823 2017 | DDC 202/.11—dc23

Printed in China

10 9 8 7 6 5 4 3 2 1

BOOK DESIGN BY KATY RIEGEL WITH ALISSA ROSE THEODOR

Essential Truths

God is communicating
with us all the time.

QUESTION

How do I know God is communicating with me?

ANSWER

Because God reaffirms . . .

"I talk to everyone. All the time. The question is not to whom do I talk, but who listens? The whole universe will I use to do this.

So be on the lookout. Watch, listen.

The words to the next song you hear.

The information in the next article you read.

The story line of the next movie you watch.

The chance utterance of the next person you meet. Or the whisper of the next river, the next ocean, the next breeze that caresses your ear—all these devices are Mine; all these avenues are open to Me.

I will speak to you if you will listen." Through thoughts, feelings, experience and words. "I will come to you if you will invite Me."

However, God reminds us that his first tool is "the voice within you . . . because it is the most accessible." The voice within is the loudest voice with which I speak, because it is the closest to you. It is the voice which tells you whether everything else is true or false, right or wrong, good or bad as you have defined it. It is the radar that sets the course, steers the ship, guides the journey if you but let it.

So stay awake, for God will "bring you the exact right thoughts, words, or feelings, at any given moment, suited precisely to the purpose at hand."

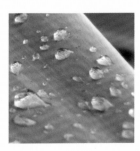

Feeling is the language of the soul.

QUESTION

Should I always trust my feelings?

ANSWER

Feelings reside in the soul and the soul is God-in-you. In this place is your truth, and it is in no other. God says that if you want to know what's true for you about something, look to how you're feeling about it.

Your feelings are what you know about a thing. Your feeling is your truth. It is exactly how you feel about a thing, based on what you factually and intuitively know. However, because feelings are what you know about a thing, although they will always be your truth, they may not be the truth about something; for instance, people once felt the world was "flat."

Be aware that data reside in the mind and are not a feeling. So knowing the difference between messages from God and data from other sources is a simple matter of applying a basic rule.

God explains this rule:

"Mine is always your Highest Thought, your Clearest Word, your Grandest Feeling. Anything less is from another source." So trust your *grandest* feelings, for God says, "My most common form of communication is through feeling."

I cannot tell you
My Truth

until you stop telling Me yours.

Thought,
Word, and Deed are the
three levels of creation.

QUESTION

How is it that Thought, Word, and Deed are the three levels of creation?

ANSWER

It has been said that you create in your mind. And that is true. You create in your mind with the energy of your thought. The mind does not create, but thought does.

God explains that "every prayer—every thought, every statement, every feeling—is creative."

Your thought, word and of course deeds are all actions. The moment you think, you speak, you do something, you create something. Your thoughts, your words, your deeds all create with the energy which you are. "Thought is pure energy. Every thought you have, have ever had, and ever will have is creative."

In fact, "Natural Law requires the body, mind, and spirit to be united in thought, word, and action for the process of creation to work." So the key here is to get out of your mind (your ego) and search your soul, in order to know and create from your Highest Thoughts, because "you are the creator of your reality, and life can show up no other way for you than that way in which you think it will."

FEAR

is the energy which contracts,

closes down, draws in,

runs, hides,

hoards, harms.

LOVE

is the energy which expands,
opens up, sends out, stays,
reveals, shares, heals.

There are only two Sponsoring
Thoughts: fear and love.

QUESTION

Why are our Sponsoring Thoughts so important?

ANSWER

Every human thought and every human action is based in either love or fear. Our ideas, decisions, and actions emerge from one of these two energies. The polarity between love and fear forms the basis of the Law of Opposites, which law is obeyed by all of life in the physical realm.

Because thought is creative, your first thought or first serious thought you ever had about a thing usually becomes your Sponsoring Thought about that thing, and it in turn creates your reality. For example, believing in the false thought that: God is the creator and decider of all things in your life.

God explains . . . "What you must know (and here is the secret)—is that it is the thought behind the thought (what might be called the Sponsoring Thought)—that is the controlling thought." The key to our level of consciousness is our awareness of these Sponsoring Thoughts.

So as you travel through your every day, be aware of whether your thoughts are being sponsored by the uplifting energy of love or the debilitating energy of fear. Because "thoughts rooted in fear will produce one kind of manifestation on the physical plane, whilst thoughts rooted in love will produce another." We need to choose those thoughts rooted in love, in every instant, in every moment, in every circumstance. Love is the highest thought. And it is easy to choose, because it is always that thought which contains joy!

In the absence of that which you
are not, that which you are . . .
is not.

QUESTION

Why, in the absence of that which you are not, that which you are . . . is not?

ANSWER

Because . . . a thing cannot exist without its opposite, except in the world of the Absolute. "In the Absolute there is no experience, only knowing." Knowing something and experiencing it are two different things.

Thus the physical universe was created as a realm within which we might experience ourselves as that which we Really Are, through the experiencing of that which we are not. God reaffirms this: "Once in the physical universe, you, My spirit children, could experience what you know of yourself (conceptually)—but first you had to come to know the opposite."

All things in the physical realm exist within the Law of Opposites and are defined by what they are not. The Law states that you cannot "be" a thing in the absence of that thing which you are not being. Thankfully, "You do not have to create the opposite of Who You Are and What you Choose in order to experience it. You merely need to observe that it has already been created—elsewhere—and remember that it exists."

Ironically, the moment you declare yourself to be anything, everything unlike it will come into your life. This is the Law of Opposites at work. And so, a totally new way of behaving needs to occur so the problem goes away and a new situation is consciously created. When you do this, you decide who you choose to Be, and that new person will be a magnificent Conscious Creator who observes "what is so" and chooses "what works."

The correct prayer is . . .
never a prayer of
supplication, but
a prayer of gratitude.

There is no such thing as "right" and "wrong."

QUESTION

How can there be no such thing as "right" and "wrong"?

ANSWER

Gods tells us that "I have never set down a 'right' or 'wrong,' a 'do' or a 'don't.' To do so would strip you completely of your greatest gift—the opportunity to do as you please, and experience the results of that; the chance to create yourself anew in the image and likeness of Who You Really Are; the space to produce a reality of a higher and higher you, based on your grandest idea of what it is of which you are capable."

"Rightness" or "wrongness" is not an intrinsic condition, it is a subjective judgment in a personal value system. By your subjective judgments do you create your Self—by your personal values do you determine and demonstrate Who You Are.

God has given us free will and there are no demands in life—not from God. There are no "shoulds" or "shouldnt's" in God's world, either. "I will give you whatever you call forth, whether it's good for you or bad for you."

However, although God tells us to "do what you want to do," He encourages us to "do what reflects you, what re-presents you as a grander version of your Self." Regardless of our choice, though, no matter what we do, God doesn't give a damn—all He gives are blessings. It is we who need to determine what is our highest choice and choose that.

19

A thing is only right or wrong because you say it is.

All attack is a call for help.

What you fear,

you attract.

QUESTION

Why is it that what you fear, you attract?

ANSWER

Because "all physical life functions in accordance with natural Laws and the Second Law (of the Universe) is that you attract what you fear. Even though it is hard to understand its complex implication, we need to embrace its truth and perfection in our reality.

Fear is an emotion. "Emotion is energy in motion. When you move energy, you create effect. Emotion is the power which attracts, so, that which you fear strongly, you will experience," because like energy attracts like energy—it is Law.

It is without a doubt demonstrably true that what you fear, you attract. What you fear most is what will most plague you. Your fear will draw it to you like a magnet.

Fear of God produces fear of life itself.

Fear attacks your body at a cellular level.

Fear causes us to deny Who We Really Are.

Fear is worry magnified and is the opposite of everything that you are—which is love.

So as you go through life, it is important to know the difference between fear and caution. Fear immobilizes, caution empowers. So take natural precautions, but do not allow fear to paralyze. For it is as God says: "Man cannot discover new oceans until he is prepared to lose sight of the shore."

There is only one reason to do anything: as a statement to the universe of Who You Are.

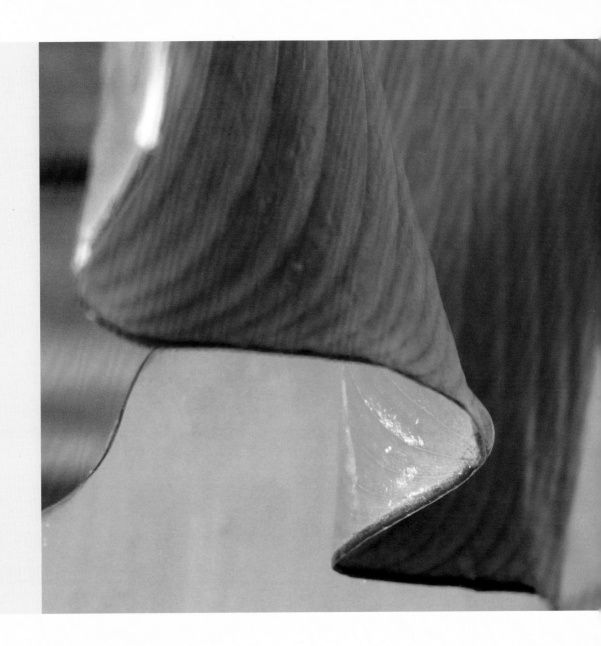

God is Life,
and the Stuff Life Is.

QUESTION

Who is God?

ANSWER

The identity, appearance, and messages of God are right in front of us all the time. Who is God? "God is everything." God is All That Is and All That Is Not. But God tells us that "if you think God looks only one way, or sounds only one way, or is only one way, you're going to look right past Me night and day."

God explains that "there is a divine purpose behind everything—and therefore a divine presence in everything. So, God is in the profane and the profound, God is the up and the down. The hot and the cold. The left and the right. The reverent and the irreverent!"

With God you can laugh, enjoy a good joke, use slang words or tough language. God tells us that "I despise nothing. None of it is repulsive to Me. It is life, and life is the gift, the unspeakable treasure, the holy of holies."

Who is God? "God is more than you imagine. God is the energy you call imagination. God is creation. God is first thought. God is last experience. And God is everything in between." God explains that "each of you has your own construction. Each of you has understood Me—created Me—in your own way. To some of you I am a man. To some of you I am a woman. To some, I am both. To some, I am neither. To some of you I am pure energy. To some, the ultimate feeling, which you call love. And some of you have no idea what I am. You simply know that I AM."

No matter what we believe God to be, one thing is true—God is Life, and all the Stuff That Life Is!

God needs nothing,
and therefore requires
nothing from us.

QUESTION

Why doesn't God need or require anything from us?

ANSWER

Because Deity (God), the All That Is, is exactly that—all that there is. She therefore wants, or lacks, nothing. There is nothing that He is not, so what could He possibly want? God assures us that "I do not want your worship, I do not need your obedience, and it is not necessary for you to serve Me." If God did need anything, he tells us, that would make us Children of a Lesser God. He tells us again that "I am without needs. I require nothing!"

God does, however, have desires. A desire is something you choose to have. It is a preference. Whereas a "need" is something you must have. God explains that His second desire is "that you shall know and experience Who You Really Are, through the power I have given you to create and experience yourself in whatever way you choose."

The concept of a God who has needs and requires us to obey His commands is counterfeit. Our God has desires, not needs. Ours is not an angry, demanding, jealous, or retributive God—ours is a joyful, loving, accepting, blessing, grateful God . . . our God is a God to fall in love with!

Allow each soul
to walk its path.

If you do not go within,
you go without.

God talks to everyone.

QUESTION

If God talks to everyone, does that include me?

ANSWER

"Many people choose to believe that God communicates in special ways and only with special people. There is no person and there is no time one more special than another. All people are special, and all moments are golden." Listening to what other people think they have heard God say is the biggest reason most people turn away from believing they are receiving God's messages directly.

"This is the root of every problem you experience in your life—for you do not consider yourself worthy enough to be spoken to by God. Good heavens, how can you ever expect to hear My voice if you don't imagine yourself deserving enough to ever be spoken to?"

God invites us to start a new, earnest communication with Him now and says, "I will bring you the exact right thoughts, words, or feelings, at any given moment, suited precisely to the purpose at hand, using one device, or several." God reiterates that books are not the only way She speaks, and says, "Listen to Me in the truth of your soul. Listen to Me in the feelings of your heart. Listen to Me in the quiet of your mind. Hear Me, everywhere."

God's response could be in an article you read, the sermon you hear, a movie you see, in a song, in the words of a loved one, or in the heart of a friend.

Yes, God does talk to everyone, and "some will be able to hear—and some will be able to only listen, but will hear nothing."

Human beings
consist of three
distinct energies.

QUESTION

If human beings consist of three distinct energies, what are they?

ANSWER

God explains, "You are a threefold being. You consist of body, mind, and spirit. You could also call these the physical, the nonphysical, and the metaphysical. This is the Holy Trinity, and it has been called by many names. That which you are, I am, I am manifested as Three-in-One. Some of your theologies have called this Father, Son, and Holy Spirit."

These three energies are our creative tools. They are the divine devices with which God has made it possible for us to fashion the fabric of our experience—you might call them thought, word, and action or deed. God explains, "All three put together produce a result—which in your language and understanding is called a feeling, or experience. Your Soul (subconscious, spirit) is the sum total of every feeling you've ever had."

When we comprehend that nothing exists in the world which did not first exist as pure thought, we understand that throughout our life, we are operating within the framework of an immutable law which states that how you think, speak, and act will be reflected in your reality. When you live as a three-part being, not only do you work with the creative law of the universe, you come at last into balance with yourself. Also, as human beings are made in the "image and likeness of God," it stands to reason that as we are in the process of experiencing ourselves by creating ourselves anew in every single moment, so, too, is God, through each one of us. God says, "It is a holy collaboration—truly!"

And so we see that the Beginning is God. Then the three levels of creation came together through ideas forming, thought being expressed, and words moving in action. The End result is the experience of God and human beings.

All you see in your world
is the outcome of your
idea about it.

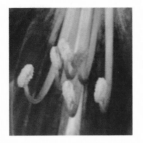

QUESTION

Why is it that all we see in our world is the outcome of our idea about it?

ANSWER

It's because our ideas about the things in our world are really outcomes of the thoughts we have about those things. "The process of creation starts with thought—an idea, conception, visualization. Everything you see was once someone's idea. Nothing exists in your world that did not first exist as pure thought." So it becomes extremely advantageous for us to go immediately to our highest thought about everything, and everyone, important to us, if we are to create our personal world the way we want to see it.

God explains that "if you are God's equal, that means nothing is being done to you—and all things are created by you." So, "There can be no more victims and no more villains—only outcomes of your thought about a thing."

If you "want your life to truly take off, then instead of experiencing the aftermath of your unconscious creation, change your idea about it. About you. Think, speak, and act as the God You Are by consciously changing everything you think, everything you say, and everything you do that is not in alignment or harmony with the highest vision you have of you. . . . When you do a thing that is misaligned with your best intention, decide then and there to make that the last time." Begin to use the three tools of creation, to change and call a stop to unconscious living.

LOVE

is the ultimate reality.

It is the only.

The all.

The feeling of love is your

experience of God.

All conditions are temporary.

Nothing stays the same.

QUESTION

How can all conditions be temporary and nothing stays the same?

ANSWER

Because it is possible for you to think thoughts, say words, and undertake deeds which are not reactions, but are creations—deliberate creations—and it is by this process that you change your life. To a very large degree it could be said that the quality of your life will depend upon the degree to which you control or create the changes which affect it.

To create and not react, you need to "go to your Highest Thought about yourself. Imagine the you that you would be if you lived that thought every day. Imagine what you would think, do, and say, and how you would respond to what others do and say. Do you see the difference between that projection and what you think, do, and say now?"

Remember that all you see in your world is the outcome of your idea about it. You have created your entire reality, but what is important for you to understand is that you do have the opportunity to choose again. Because nothing remains the same. Nothing. Not even God.

And so we see that all conditions must be temporary and nothing can stay the same. For that is the purpose of life and it is called evolution.

The purpose of
the soul is evolution.

QUESTION

Why is the purpose of the soul evolution?

ANSWER

Because "what the soul is after is—the highest feeling of love you can imagine," and because "the highest feeling is the experience of unity with All That Is, for the soul to experience perfect love, it must experience every human feeling." So to evolve in this world of relativity, change is not only inevitable, it is desirable, for the Soul must ultimately experience all of it in order to experience itself as any of it and fully realize itself while in the body.

God says that "we can see both the simplicity and the awesome magnitude of the soul's journey when we understand at last what it is up to" and see how "the Law of Opposites plays its effect in our lives, assisting us in creating, being, and experiencing Who We Really Are. How can it be up if it has never been down, left if it has never been right? How can it be warm if it knows not cold, good if it denies evil? Obviously, the Soul cannot choose to be anything if there is nothing to choose from," and so, for the soul to evolve through the body, it needs change.

"The soul is very clear that its purpose is evolution . . . it is not concerned with the achievements of the body or the development of the mind. These are all meaningless to the soul." Your soul's agenda is seeking to be God in its own experience and it does this by urging you to choose the very best of Who You Are. "This is a big task, taking many lifetimes." It is through this deep understanding that we see "the soul is also very clear that there is no great tragedy involved in leaving the body. In many ways the tragedy is being in the body. So you have to understand, the soul sees this whole death thing differently."

Constant change is the point of all life and underpins the soul's purpose and journey upward, what we know as evolution: knowing, experiencing, being.

I have established Laws in the universe that make it possible for you to have—to create—exactly what you choose.

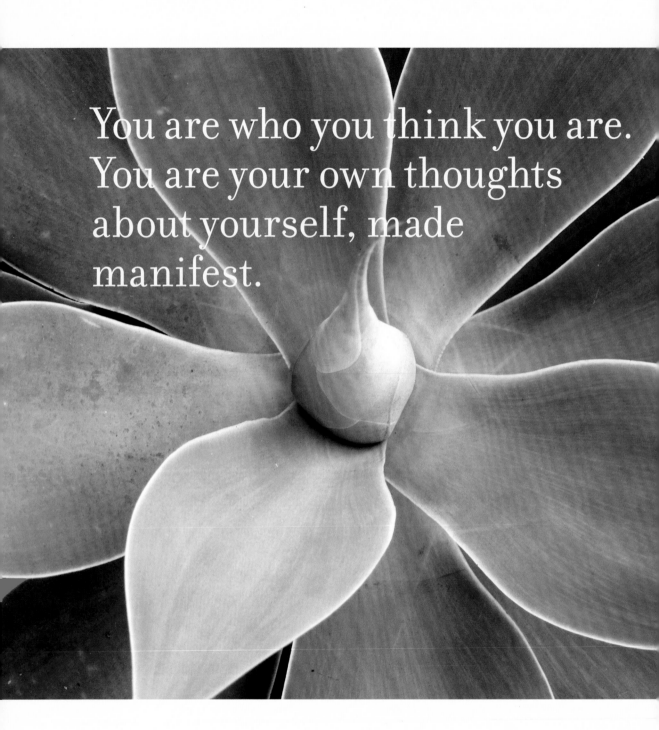

You are who you think you are. You are your own thoughts about yourself, made manifest.

QUESTION

So, who am I really?

ANSWER

You are many extraordinary things right now, and I can assure you: who you think you are is exactly who you will wind up being.

Sadly, most people hold the thought that they are inherently "bad" and that almost everything they desire, or that brings them enjoyment in life, is also bad. So God tells us again, even though we continue not to accept it: "You are born of God, you are pure Gods and Goddesses at birth." Every Master has brought us this same message from God: "What I am, you are." God knows us as this, and says that "if you saw you as God sees you, you'd smile a lot." Most people do not see themselves as God knows them to be.

Most people do not see themselves as being the way God knows them to be. Instead we have chosen to think much less of ourselves, and there's a very large "gap" between who we think we are and Who We Really Are.

God tells us: "You are goodness and mercy and compassion and understanding. You are peace and joy and light. You are forgiveness and patience, strength and courage, a helper in time of need, a comforter in time of sorrow, a healer in time of injury, a teacher in times of confusion. You are the deepest wisdom and the highest truth; the greatest peace and the grandest love. You are these things, and in moments of your life you have known yourself as these things."

It's time to see yourself the way God sees you and "choose now to know yourself as these things always," for you truly are magnificent!

The purpose of the

human soul is

to experience

all of it—

so that it can **be** all of it.

Life is not a process of discovery,
it is a process of creation.

QUESTION

Why is life a process of creation and not a
process of discovery?

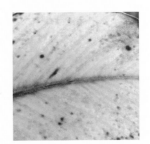

ANSWER

Because there is nothing new to learn, "you need merely remember what you already know,
and act on it." We have it all backward: "You are not discovering yourself, but creating yourself anew." You do not live each day to discover what it holds for you, but to create it. You are
creating your reality every minute, probably without knowing it. You are here "to remember,
and re-create, Who You Are." Here's why that is so, and how it works.

God's Ten-Point Path to Realization of Self as Creator (in short). Commit these to memory
so you will no longer be sleepwalking through your life but will be consciously aware of what
you are thinking, saying, and doing—and of the impact that is having in your life.

1. I have created you in the image and likeness of God.
2. God is the creator.
3. You are three beings in one.
4. Creation is a process, which proceeds from these three parts of your body—the tools are:
   thought, word, and deed.
5. All creation begins with thought, then moves to word, and is fulfilled in deed.
6. Thought creates at one level, thought and word at another, and thought, word, and action
   become manifest.
7. The process of creation must include belief or knowing (faith).
8. Knowing is incredible gratitude (thankfulness in advance)—the biggest key to creation,
   which all Masters know.
9. Celebrate and enjoy all that you create, have created. Own it, claim it, bless it, be thankful
   for it.
10. If there is any aspect of creation you do not enjoy, bless it and simply change it by choosing
    again, calling forth a new reality.

"You can train yourself to do this. Look how well you've trained yourself not to do it."

There is no such thing as the Ten Commandments.

QUESTION

How can there be no such thing as the Ten Commandments?

ANSWER

Because "the word of God is not a commandment, but a covenant." God asks, "Who would I command? Myself? And why would such commandments be required? Whatever I want, is. Isn't that so? How is it therefore necessary to command anyone? . . . And who shall I punish should My commandments not be kept? There is only Me."

God declares that "He is neither a king nor a ruler, but simply, and awesomely, the Creator. And as the Creator, God performs one function only—She creates, creates, and keeps on creating. . . . I have created you—blessed you—in the image and likeness of Me. And I have made certain promises and commitments to you. I have told you how it will be when you become at one with Me."

And so, God has given us his Ten Commitments, saying that "you shall know that you have taken the path to God . . . found God, for there will be these signs . . . indications . . . these changes in you. These are your freedoms, not your restrictions. These are my commitments, not my commandments. And they are (in short):

1. You shall love God with all your heart . . . mind . . . soul.
2. You shall not use the name of God in vain.
3. You shall remember to keep a day for Me . . . and . . . call it holy.
4. You shall honor your mother and your father.
5. You will not murder . . . (but) will . . . honor all life-forms.
6. You will not defile the purity of love with dishonesty or deceit.
7. You will not take a thing that is not your own, nor cheat . . . harm another to have any thing . . . Nor shall you . . .
8. Say a thing that is not true . . .
9. Covet your neighbor's spouse . . .
10. Covet your neighbor's goods . . .

"For God does not order about what God has created—God merely tells God's children (through signs) this is how you know that you are coming home."

In order to truly
know God,
you have to be out
of your mind.

What you
resist persists.

56

QUESTION

Why does what you resist persist?

ANSWER

Because "the act of resisting a thing is the act of granting it life. When you resist an energy, you place it there. The more you resist, the more you make it real—whatever it is you are resisting." And this is so because you cannot resist something which does not exist. In fact, your very resistance to something is an announcement to the universe that you believe it is there. And, of course, what you believe is what will be made manifest in your reality.

"Remember, you are constantly in the act of creating yourself. You are in every moment deciding who and what you are. You decide this largely through the choices you make regarding who and what you feel passionate about." Therefore, passions are not to be avoided. Indeed, it is passion which drives the engine of the human experience, depending upon what it is you are trying to do or be. Don't resist your passion for a thing, simply notice it, then look to see if it serves you to indulge in it now—or ever. Do not renounce (give up), judge, or condemn a thing, either, for to do so is to condemn the creation and thus the Creator.

A Master understands this and does not condemn, nor "give up" earthly passion or desire, he merely sets it aside, steps around it, "all the while loving the illusion for what it has brought to him: the chance to be wholly free," and thus free of the attachment to results.

As our choices are unrestricted, our opportunities unlimited, and our paths unending, do not try to resist your most passionate urges and desires, for it will not work. Instead, look to see which passions serve you, help you to achieve a goal, bring you joy, goodness, and benefit. And when you see those that do not serve you, choose to step around them, and, in doing so, express and declare Who You Truly Want to Be.

Enlightenment is understanding that there is nowhere to go, nothing to do, and nobody you have to be except exactly who you're being right now.

Passion is not expectation,
and expectation
is not passion.

QUESTION

Why is passion not expectation and expectation not passion?

ANSWER

Because "passion is the love of turning being into action. It fuels the engine of creation. It changes concepts to experience . . . it is the fire that drives us to express who we really are. Passion is a love of doing, and doing is being, experienced. Passion is God wanting to say, Hi!"

Yet what is often created as part of doing is—expectation. Expectation is the need for specific results from your actions. God tells us that "expectation—is the greatest source of man's unhappiness. To live your life without expectation, without the need for specific results—that is freedom."

So often, when man is motivated to do something loving, he expects to get something back in return, which generally ruins whatever he may have had a passion for in the beginning. In other words, man often feels he needs a return on his investment. On the other hand, when "God (God-in-you) does that loving thing, God has realized Itself, and needs nothing more."

So, "Never deny passion, for that is to deny Who You Are, and Who You Truly Want to Be. The renunciate never denies passion, the renunciate simply denies attachment to results."

Suffering is not necessary.

QUESTION

How can it be true that suffering is not necessary?

ANSWER

In truth, and although it is difficult to believe and accept—suffering is a point of view! Suffering is caused, in fact, by your reaction to something.

God tells us, "Suffering is an unnecessary aspect of the human experience. It is not only unnecessary, it is unwise, uncomfortable, and hazardous to your health." It is our judgments (often based on previous experience) and our expectations (attachment to results) that begin our suffering. "Suffering has nothing to do with events, but one's reaction to them. What's happening is merely what's happening. How you feel about it is another matter."

The events in our lives which we believe cause our suffering "are occurrences in time and space which you produce out of choice." God has "given us the tools with which to respond and react to events in a way which reduces—in fact, eliminates—pain, but we have not used them. You cannot change the outer event . . . so you must change the inner experience . . . Nothing is painful in and of itself. Pain is a result of wrong thought. It is an error in thinking."

God explains that "some events you produce willfully and some events you draw to you—more or less unconsciously." In other words, we draw to us that which we pay attention to, and it becomes our reality. So it makes sense that when you are "experiencing a set of circumstances that you would call insufferable," you choose to experience something else. The Master clearly understands this and places himself at choice with regard to that which he chooses to make real, because what you give your attention to—you make real.

Suffering is not necessary, indeed suffering is not real, it is your decision about a thing—it is a point of view!

What's
happening
is merely
what's
happening.

How
you feel
about it is
another matter.

You need no God.

QUESTION

How could we not need God?

ANSWER

We often turn to God and ask Him to be there for us in times of need. But the reason that we don't need God's help is that we already, and always, have it. Anyone who wears glasses has at least once in their life gone looking for their glasses . . . while wearing them. It happens to everyone. We simply forget we are wearing them. We sometimes forget that God is acting as us, in us, through us all the time—so we don't need what we already have.

When God says "you need no God," it seems like an astonishing statement. But in fact, God tells us that "God's greatest moment is the moment you realize you need no God," for when you understand this, you acknowledge that it is possible precisely because of God's ever-present existence within us, ready to serve us in any and every moment.

For "a true God is not One with the most servants, but One who serves the most, thereby making Gods of all others." God acknowledges that "it is a great challenge, this path of the householder. There are many distractions, many worldly concerns," and She invites us to recognize the presence of God in every moment.

So how do we "play this spiritual game," committing to creating Self in the image and likeness of God and putting an end to our illusion of a need for God? God reminds us that "this is a day-to-day, hour-to-hour, moment-to-moment act of supreme consciousness. It is a choosing and a re-choosing every instant. It is ongoing creation. Conscious creation. Creation with a purpose. It is using the tools of creation with awareness and sublime intention." This is the process of self-realization.

Although this path requires constant dedication, you will find that happiness and abundance follow as a natural consequence of your spiritual wisdom and clarity.

Your Life is always a result of your

thoughts about it—including your

obviously creative thought

that you seldom

get what you

choose.

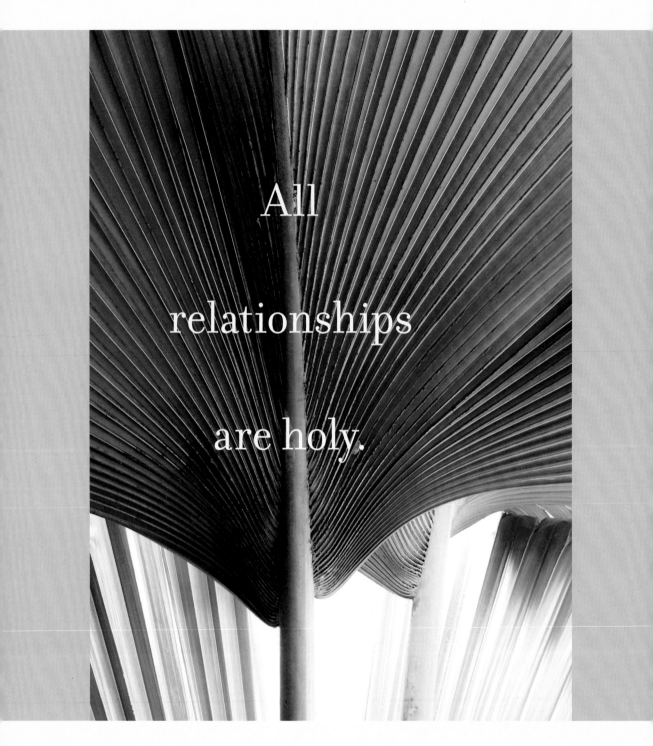

All

relationships

are holy.

QUESTION

Why are all relationships holy?

ANSWER

Because every relationship, with every person, place, or thing, allows you to . . . be and to declare, to become and to fulfill, to express and to experience Who You Really Are. Every relationship is a blessed gift—even those which bring sadness and pain. Without relationships we are nothing, because we can only experience ourselves in relation to something or someone else. Personal relationships are the most important elements in this process and are therefore holy ground."

Romantic relationships are sacred "because they provide life's grandest opportunity—indeed, its only opportunity—to create and produce the experience of your highest conceptualization of Self. God says that the most loving person is the person who is Self-centered. For if you cannot love your Self, you cannot love another, and many people make the mistake of seeking love of Self through love for another. And so, "Most people enter relationships with an eye toward what they can get out of them, rather than what they can put into them. The purpose of relationship is to decide what part of yourself you'd like to see show up, not what part of another you can capture and hold." This is why so many relationships break down. People go into them for the wrong reason—to end loneliness, bring themselves love. They believe that their special other will make them feel complete, yet the purpose is to have another with whom you might share your completeness.

God says that the problem is so basic, so simple, and yet so tragically misunderstood. The true test of a relationship is how will you live up to your grandest dream, your highest idea, your fondest hope of your beloved Self. He encourages us to "do whatever you do out of a sense of the glorious opportunity your relationship affords you to decide, and to be, Who You Really Are—the God-in-you. And he reminds us that to do this, firstly you must learn to honor, and cherish, and love your Self—for it is Soul Work that you are up to!

Your purpose in life is to decide and to declare, to express and to experience, Who You Really Are; this is the purpose of ALL of life; that is evolution.

QUESTION

How can I live my purpose in life?

ANSWER

You do that by living "the grandest version of the greatest vision" you ever had about yourself. It's that standard against which you can measure everything you think, say, and do. In other words, when deciding how to act or re-act to any situation, ask yourself beforehand: Is this thing I am now thinking, now saying, or now doing, a reflection of the grandest version of the greatest vision I've ever had about myself? Because by this you define the richest definition of yourself you can imagine. You not only decide to be the best you can be, but you touch the lives of all others you contact with happiness, goodness, and purpose. You see, when your idea about yourself is very high, and when you do nothing all day long but serve that idea, you cannot but be a blessing to others. In fact, we are the highest blessing to others when we serve the highest calling within ourselves.

When you are very centered in this "space," it could be said that you are being very self-centered, by putting yourself first. However God tells us, "Let each person in relationship worry not about the other, but only, only, only about the Self . . . the most loving person is the person who is Self-centered." The Master knows that it isn't about what any other is being, doing, having, saying, wanting, or demanding. It only matters what you are being in relationship to that. So understand "it is not in the action of another, but in your re-action, that your salvation will be found."

When you are truly serious about the purpose of life, you will go out and walk your talk. You will seek to live this "grandest version" of Who You Are. For God has told us over and over again "to remember, and re-create, Who You Are. For truly, if you do not create yourself as Who You Are, that you cannot be."

The trick is to see the game and enjoy the process!

Let each person

in relationship

worry not about

the other,

74

but only, only, only about the Self.

Relationships work best when you

always do what is best for you.

QUESTION

Why should I always do what is best for me in my relationships?

ANSWER

Because "the highest good for you becomes the highest good for another."

God explains that, sadly, "for centuries you have been taught that love-sponsored action arises out of the choice to be, do, and have whatever produces the highest good for another . . . however, the highest choice is that which produces the highest good for you. And "this truth revolves around an even greater one: What you do for your Self, you do for another. What you do for another, you do for the Self. This is because you and the other are one. And this is because . . . there is naught but You."

Indeed, "God suggests—recommends—that you put yourself first." And assures us that when you remain self-centered and always focused on what is best for you, you will never perform an ungodly act. In fact, if you refuse to deviate from your process of re-creating yourself anew in every moment of Now in the next grandest version of the greatest vision You ever held about Who You Are, you will never dis-serve another by serving yourself.

Your purpose is therefore to remain singularly focused. However, if "you have caught yourself in an ungodly act as a result of doing what is best for you, the confusion is not in having put yourself first, but rather in misunderstanding what is best for you." So how do you do what is best for you? You move through your relationships, both personal and business, with the clarity that you have no obligations to "have to do" anything other than what you feel you choose to do, out of your decision about Who You Are and what you choose to be, do, and have in your life.

It is not
in the action
of another,

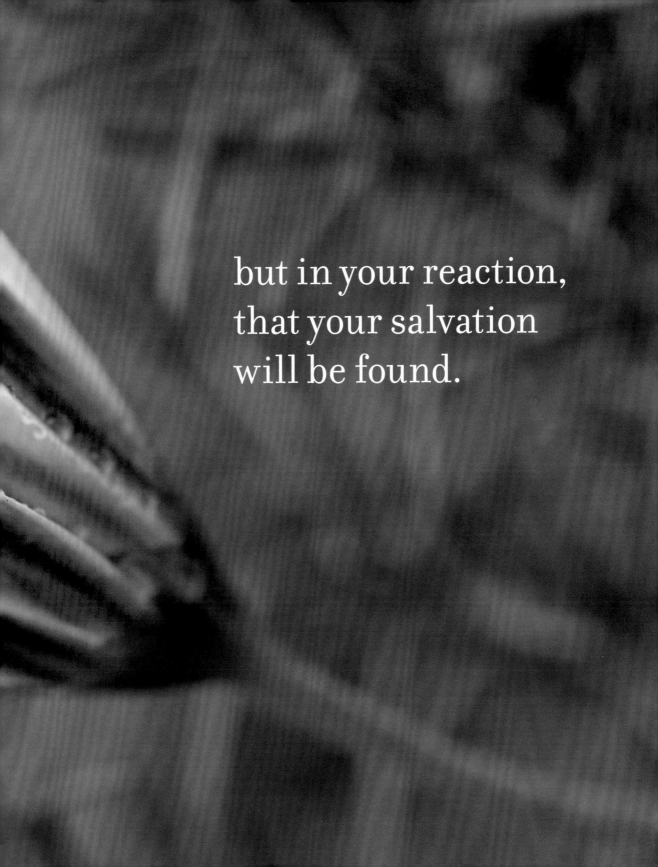

but in your reaction,
that your salvation
will be found.

You are a messenger.

QUESTION

What am I a messenger of?

ANSWER

Every day, every moment, with every thought you think, word you speak, and deed you do, you send a message to the universe, to God, and to all those whose lives you touch: This is Who I Am! Yet not only is your message This is Who I Am. It is also, this is who you can be. For you are setting an example, showing the way: "I am the Life and the Way," you are saying. "Follow me." You have come as a savior. You have not come here to be saved, but to save others. That is why it is so important to work on yourself.

You have nothing to learn, you have only to re-member, that is, become a member once again of the Body of God. You were also not sent here to take care of "you," or somehow solve your problems. You were given these problems as gifts, divine opportunities to choose and declare, express and experience, know and fulfill Who You Really Are, so that in the knowing you could show others who do not know. That is your assignment and that is the great secret. So, everything we think, say, and do sends a message to someone about Who We Are, and that message reaffirms to others Who They Are. What they see in you is a mirror image of themselves.

However, God warns us that our personal relationships, from which we experience our greatest pain and suffering, and our most joy, may not be easy. In fact, God says, "Know and understand that there will be challenges and difficult times. Don't try to avoid them. Welcome them. Gratefully. See them as grand gifts from God; glorious opportunities to do what you came into the relationship—and life—to do." And so, a long and happy relationship shared with another is one that is entered into for the right reasons—mutual growth, mutual expression, and mutual fulfillment. "Marriage is therefore a glorious and unequaled opportunity to express your highest self, and demonstrate your purpose in life, which is to be Who You Really Are." In all relationships, especially marriage, you are a messenger saying, This is Who I Am—so strive to show your beloved the very best version of you.

There is naught

but You.

You Are the Truth.

QUESTION

What does "I Am the Truth" mean?

ANSWER

Firstly, understand—what you define as right or wrong (in your reality, right here, right now), you do so as a definition of yourself, as Who You Have Become from the totality of your experiences. The statement You Are the Truth means there is no other truth which matters but your own. There is no absolute right and wrong. What you say is right or wrong paints a portrait of Who You Are. Your challenge is in the definition of Your Self through the painting (creating) of this evolving portrait. Why? Because this portrait changes. You're always painting over, creating a new painting—this is evolution. You continually update the picture of Who You Are through the announcement of your latest decisions about what you call right and wrong.

Now, we know in Ultimate Reality there is no such thing as right and wrong, but what we are talking about here is whether we are making our choices and decisions based on someone else's truth of right and wrong, or on our own. And this is pointed out in God's question: "And what, pray tell, forms the basis of your decision? Your own experience? No. In most cases you've chosen to accept someone else's decision. Someone who came before you and, presumably, knows better . . . This is especially true on important matters. In fact, the more important the matter, the less likely you are to listen to your own experience, and the more ready you seem to be to make someone else's ideas your own." When we allow the truth of others to define us, we are engaging in unconscious self-creation. For centuries our country, religions, and societies have needed us to believe their truth in order for them to survive.

Sadly, most of your life you have been defining yourself unconsciously, by going to your memory bank and retrieving what someone else has told you about life. Instead, God invites you to avoid automatic reactions which tend to create you as who you were, rather than who you now choose to be. Go inside and see what is true for you now in your present reality, remembering that everything you think, say, and do is an act of self-definition. Step into conscious creation by taking a second to stop and think: Is this Who I Now Am?

God's love is unconditional.

QUESTION

Why do we find unconditional love so hard to believe and accept?

ANSWER

Because, God tells us, "It was your parents (whom you dearly loved) who taught you that love is conditional, and because you have felt their conditions many times, that is the experience you take into your own love relationships. It is also the experience you bring to Me, and draw your conclusions about Me. Within this framework you speak your truth that God is a loving God, but if you break His commandments, He will punish you with eternal banishment and everlasting damnation."

As we have experienced the banishment of our parents and the pain of their damnation, we imagine it to be the same with God. We have thus projected the role of parent onto God, and come up with the belief that God judges, rewards, or punishes us based on how good He feels about what we've been up to. We have "created an entire thought system about God based on human experience, rather than spiritual truths," and an entire reality around love which is fear-based, and rooted in the idea of a vengeful God.

Yet the Truth is so natural and so simple—God loves us, and that love is unconditional. But "by your own (mistaken) thoughts about love do you damn yourself never to experience it purely." God says, "You do not remember the experience of the love of God. And so you try to imagine what God's love must be like, based on what you see of love in the world." Yet God's love is not like the love we find in the world, because God's love is without conditions. What could be more perfect? What could be more comforting?

And so, as we journey through the critical junctures of our own human relationships in life, it would be good for us to remember that there is only one question we should ask ourselves. And that is: What would love do now?

For most people,
love is a response
to need fulfillment.

There's enough.

QUESTION

If there is enough, then why don't I see this in my world?

ANSWER

Everything we are fighting about or have ever fought over on this planet has, as its base, the root thought that there is something of which there is not enough. Wars are fought either because I'm protecting my "stuff" or I'm wanting the "stuff" that's yours. And the reason behind each is that both sides believe there is not enough stuff to go around for everybody. Sadly, it is a lack of the will to share that is the problem, not a lack of the stuff to share. Because if everybody simply came to each human encounter with the "there's enough" attitude and understanding, those encounters would be less defensive, less destructive, and human suffering would end. If this one single Truth—"there's enough"—was deeply understood and firmly held in consciousness it could change the world.

On a personal level, this race consciousness of "not-enoughness" creates and re-creates the world as we see it. God says, "In fact, you have this root thought about just about everything. There's not enough money, there's not enough time, there's not enough love, food, water, compassion in the world . . . whatever there is that's good, there's just not enough."

Few energies within the personal life experience affect us quite like money. In short, what is needed to reverse the fortunes in your life is to reverse your values around money and the belief system they have sponsored. To turn your life around—turn your values around.

First, begin to value more monetarily those things which you value highly intrinsically—and demonstrate that.

Next, reverse your thought about what you believe your worth to be—then double it.

Then, choose to receive from the universe all that you are worth in multiple ways.

Lastly, give some money away and then watch as the universal laws begin the flow of that energy right back to you.

You are a
human being.

QUESTION

What does I am a human being mean?

ANSWER

It means that your job, your "mission," your purpose on this planet, in this life, is to decide not "What are you going to do?" but "Where are you going to be?" You are a human being, not a human doing.

God tells us, "Your soul is Me, and it knows it. What it is doing is trying to experience that. And what it is remembering is that the best way to have this experience is by not doing anything. There is nothing to do but to be, whatever you want to be—happy, sad, weak, strong, joyful, vengeful, insightful, blind, good, bad, male, female. You name it!"

Doing is a function of the body. Being is a function of the soul. The body is always doing something. It's either doing what it's doing at the behest of the soul—or in spite of the soul. The quality of your life hangs in the balance. "If you think your life is about doingness, you do not understand what you are about. Your soul doesn't care what you do for a living—and when your life is over, neither will you. Your soul cares only about what you're being while you're doing whatever you're doing. It is a state of beingness the soul is after, not a state of doingness."

For many people all of life is a process of doing something in order to have something in order to be something—such as be happy, be secure, be at peace. A person can either do something in order to "be happy," or can start the day by simply deciding to "be happy," and the things that person will do will automatically reflect that. In other words, you can choose to be in any state of beingness you wish, ahead of time.

Remember, as you encounter life, that beingness attracts beingness. When you learn this, you turn your life upside down. You become a human in Conscious Creation.

True Masters

are those who

have chosen

to make a life, rather than a living.

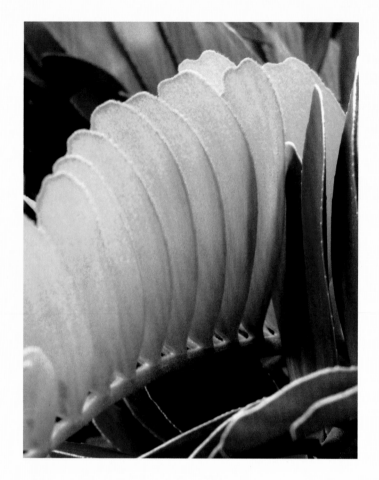

To want something is to
push it away from you.

QUESTION

Why is it true that when you want something, you push it away from you?

ANSWER

First of all, remember that your thought is creative, as are your words and actions. So if your continued thought about something is that you "want" it, and if your words about this speak of "wanting" it, and if you act as if this is something that you "want"—I want more money, I want more love, I want more peace—then the Universe has no choice but to give you the experience you have called forth . . . namely, the experience of wanting that.

God says you may not have anything you want. This is because when you, as the powerful creator that you are, make a statement to the Universe that says, "I want something," it is interpreted as a request for more of what you are currently experiencing. And what you are experiencing, right now, in your reality, is the lack of that thing.

Understand that the Universe is a big photocopier. It does not judge what you put into it, and when you program it with the powerful command "I" or "I Am," it duplicates (makes another copy) of your command. "I want love" describes yourself as currently not having love, and the Universe says, "Okay, you do" (not have love), and so you continue to experience this wantingness. That command becomes reality. "To change your reality, simply stop thinking like that. Instead of thinking, 'I want love,' think, 'I have love,' not as an affirmation which you know to be untrue, but as a statement you already know without a doubt to be true. Thank God for bringing you love from a family member, a friend, a faithful pet. Say, 'Thank you, God, for the love I have in my life.' Now, that thought, spoken and acted upon, produces wonderful results—when it comes from true knowing; not from an attempt to produce results, but from an awareness that results have already been produced." Never ask God for anything—instead, say a prayer of thanksgiving. Gratitude . . . says the Master . . . is the attitude.

"Remember, you cannot have what you want, but you may experience whatever you have." So give thanks and gratitude for what you already know you have and you will not go wanting.

If now there is something you choose to experience in your life, do not "want" it—**choose** it.

Your life is not about your body.

QUESTION

If my life is not about my body, then what is it about?

ANSWER

Your body is something you have—not something you are. Your life is about what you are, and you are a great deal more than your body. You are your body, your mind, and your soul—a combination of all three distinct characteristics. What your body is doing day today is an indication of what that combination is. If, however, you think you are your body, you will make all kinds of choices, selections, and decision which will produce little or no benefit to you.

There is not a single idea more destructive to the human race than the idea that we are only our bodies. Although, what your body is doing is a reflection of what your life is about. In fact, your body shows everyone what your life is about, but your life is not about what your body does. Your life is about what you are, and what you are becoming. And what you are is "a being in a body," who is acting out this life drama as a human being in the pursuit of remembering and becoming Who You Really Are. God explains, "There comes a time in the evolution of every soul when the chief concern is no longer the survival of the physical body, but the growth of the spirit; no longer the attainment of worldly success, but the realization of Self."

So nothing could be further from the truth than the thought that we are our bodies. And nothing could be more important for our soul than for our bodies to be a thing, do a thing, or choose to have a thing, not because of what benefit we felt it might be to our body, but because of what it might be to our soul. If our lives were about that, we would see each act as an act of self-definition, in harmony with Who We Are and who we are choosing during this lifetime to become.

Although your body is not Who You Are, it is still the Temple of your Being and should be taken care of. So honor your body—as the magnificent vehicle through which the cycle of your present life is being created, and through which the extraordinary gift of life is being experienced.

Your health is *your* creation.

QUESTION

How can my health be my creation?

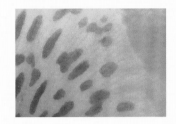

ANSWER

As a civilization, we have become complacent with our health. Many take in damaging substances regardless of copious evidence against doing so. God specifically warns us that "the body was not meant to take in alcohol, as it impairs the mind." We use the excuse of indulging only "in moderation" to justify it. And so, civilization continues to be diagnosed with chronic illness, with most people accepting no personal role in the damage to the human organism. Bad health is not something that happens to us, it happens because of us. God explains, "All illness is self-created. Even conventional medical doctors are now seeing how people make themselves sick. Most people do so quite unconsciously . . . so when they get sick, they don't know what hit them. It feels as though something has befallen them, rather than that they did something to themselves."

So yes, you create your own health, although you do so at a conscious and unconscious level. You are creating both collectively and individually, with each level of creation playing its effect on the overall experience you call life. If your individual consciousness is high enough to overcome the collective creations of humankind, or what you have been told will happen, then you can act with impunity in what you eat, drink, and do in your life and not damage your body. However, from the higher perspective, we also need to remember that "not a single thing happens in God's world which is not for good reason"—everything which occurs in the individual incarnation occurs at the behest of that soul, as a result of the creations of that soul, or of the co-creation in which it has engaged with other souls.

And so what matters is where your consciousness lies with regard to your own health. Do you take responsibility for the health of your physical body—are you treating it as the Temple of your soul? Are you a mental leper, being eaten away with negative thoughts that will translate into physical illness? And, do you make choices and exhibit behavior based on what the collective consciousness is telling you is true—or are you living your own truth? The culmination of these will determine the state of your health.

No one does anything he
doesn't want to do.

You are part of the body of God.

QUESTION

What does being part of the body of God mean for me?

ANSWER

It means that God has again explained here the ultimate mystery of our exact and true relationship to Him, and when we see this we understand the responsibility that goes with that.

Our religions have supposedly sought to unravel the mystery of our relationship with God for us, but they have generated more questions than answers and more fear of God than love of God. God says that "religion is your attempt to speak of the unspeakable. It does not do a very good job." Religion has in fact separated us from God, and yet God amazes us with the revelation: "You Are My Body . . . as your body is to your mind and soul, so, too, are you to My mind and soul. Therefore: Everything I experience, I experience through you. Just as your body, mind, and spirit are one, so, too, are Mine."

For us to comprehend this, God explains: "God is more than you imagine. God is the energy you call imagination. God is creation. God is first thought. And God is last experience. And God is everything in between. . . . All of it is God, and there is nothing else," and when we can grasp this, we understand that that also includes us! God's largest message is that all of us are Gods. "Have I not said Ye are Gods?" This revelation astounds the mind, for most of us cannot conceive of ourselves in this way.

So, each of us is in the process of growing, of becoming Who We Really Are, and there is no limit to what we can become, but accepting all of this comes with responsibility also. For now we have to drop the thought that we are a victim of an unhappy life, but the creator of it. The cause of what is going on around us, instead of being an effect of the world around us. Only then can we begin to change any of it.

We are part of the body of God and we can choose to be a bystander, or we can be "a God" and choose to make a difference in this world!

YOU ARE MY BODY.

Everything I experience,
I experience through you.

All of life is a
conversation with God.

QUESTION

How do I converse with God?

ANSWER

By knowing and understanding that God is laughing, sharing, enjoying, caring, and experiencing with you, everything, every thing in your life. Because everything in life is a conversation with God—a never-ending prayer—even those things we do in the dead of night, in the moments of our lustiest passion, as well as our most tender sharing.

God says, "You have repressed sex, even as you have repressed life, rather than fully self-expressing, with abandon and joy. You have shamed sex, even as you have shamed life, calling it evil and wicked, rather than the highest gift and the greatest pleasure." If you can imagine God in your bedroom and still be comfortable, then you can imagine God in almost any other context as well. And that is good, because God is present in every context and we would benefit from choosing to have it no other way. As you go through your day, think of your thoughts, your words, your every action as your end of a continuing Conversation with God. Because it is through these devices and in this conversation, you declare who and what you are.

Our conversation with God will never end, it can never end. God assures us that "I am always with you. . . . I will not leave you, I cannot leave you, for you are My creation and My product, My daughter and My son, My purpose and My . . . Self."

So have a conversation, a prayer that never ends with God in all that you do, and experience His presence in every aspect of your amazing life!

"I WILL NOT LEAVE YOU."

"There's a lot here to absorb. A lot to wrestle with. A lot to ponder. Take some time off. Reflect on this. Ponder it. Do not feel abandoned. I am always with you. If you have questions—day-to-day questions—as I know you do even now, and will continue to—know that you can call on Me to answer them. You do not need the form of this book.

"This is not the only way I speak to you. Listen to Me in the truth of your soul. Listen to Me in the feelings of your heart. Listen to Me in the quiet of your mind. Hear Me, everywhere. Whenever you have a question, simply know that I have answered it already. Then open your eyes to your world. My response could be in an article already published. In the sermon already written and about to be delivered. In the movie now being made. In the song just yesterday composed. In the words about to be said by a loved one. In the heart of a new friend about to be made. My truth is in the whisper of the wind, the babble of the brook, the crack of the thunder, the tap of the rain. It is the feel of the earth, the fragrance of the lily, the warmth of the sun, the pull of the moon. My truth—and your surest help in time of need—is as awesome as the night sky, and as simply, incontrovertibly trustful as a baby's gurgle. It is as loud as a pounding heartbeat—and as quiet as a breath taken in unity with Me.

"I will not leave you, I cannot leave you, for you are My creation and My product, My daughter and My son, My purpose and My . . . Self. Call on Me, therefore, wherever and whenever you are separate from the peace that I am. I will be there. With Truth. And Light. And Love."

Tell the truth.

ESSENTIAL TRUTH:

The fastest way to "find God" is to first of all understand that we and God are not apart. God is not apart from us ever, we only think we are apart from God. Sadly, we also think we're apart from each other, but we are not apart from each other, and until we know and realize that all of us are One, we cannot know and realize that we and God are One.

To find God, we need to find each other. What is required is to stop hiding out from each other and to stop hiding out from ourselves. And the fastest way to stop hiding out is to tell the truth—to everyone—all the time.

Start telling the truth now, and never stop. Begin by telling the truth to yourself about yourself. Then tell the truth to yourself about another. Then tell the truth about yourself to another. Then tell the truth about another to that other. Finally, tell the truth to everyone about everything.

Seek the truth, say the truth, live the truth every day. Do this with yourself and with every person whose life you touch.

This is the path to freedom. The truth shall set you free.

Keep

choosing

the same thing.

Essential Truth:

A secret of all Masters is to stop changing one's mind; keep choosing the same thing. Remember that life is an ongoing process of creation and you are creating your reality every minute. When you "make up your mind" about something, you set the universe in motion. Forces beyond your imagination become engaged in the process of creation, the process which we call life itself.

Therefore, be of one mind and of single purpose about a thing. And don't take your mind off it until you have produced it in your reality. Keep focused. Stay centered. This is what is meant by being single-minded. If you choose something, or have a vision, choose it with all your might, with all your heart. Don't be fainthearted. Keep going! Keep moving toward it. Be determined. Don't take no for an answer.

All of life should

be an announcement.

ESSENTIAL TRUTH:

There should be only one consideration when making any decision: Is this a statement of Who I Am? Is this an announcement of Who I Choose to Be?

All of life should be such an announcement. In fact, all of life is. You can allow that announcement to be made by chance or by choice. A life lived by choice is a life of conscious action. A life lived by chance is a life of unconscious reaction. God produces what you call forth! You call forth precisely what you think, feel, and say. It's as simple as that!

So get out of your "reactive" mind and do some "soul-searching" to create a truly genuine experience of You in the Now Moment. Decisions will be reached quickly, choices activated rapidly, because your soul creates out of present experience only, without review, analysis, and criticism of past encounters. Stop trying to figure out what is "best" for you (how you can win the most, lose the least, get what you want) and start going with what feels like Who You Are.

Release your negativities.

Essential Truth:

Feelings are neither negative nor destructive. They are simply truths.

How you express your truth is what matters. You cannot take responsibility for how well another accepts your truth; you can only ensure how well it is communicated—with love, compassion, sensitivity. So express what you call your most "negative" feelings, but not destructively.

Remember that negativity is never a sign of ultimate truth, even if it seems like your truth at the moment. It always arises out of an unhealed part of you, which is why it is so important to get these negativities out, to release them.

Failure to express (that is, push out) negative feelings does not make them go away; it keeps them in. Negativity "kept in" harms the body and burdens the soul.

Be in the moment.

Essential Truth:

There is no time but this time. There is no moment but this moment—the Eternal Moment of Now. "Now" is all there is. Everything that ever happened, is happening, and ever will happen, is happening right now.

The greatest challenge as human beings is to Be Here Now, to stop making things up—to be creative, instead of reactive. When you come to each moment cleanly, without a previous thought about it, you can create who you are, rather than reenact who you once were.

So try to ignore previous experience and go into the moment. Be Here Now. See what there is to work with right now in creating yourself anew.

Remember, this is what you are doing here. You have come to this world in this way, at this time, in this place, to know Who You Are—and to create Who You Wish to Be.

So stop creating thoughts about a pre-sent moment (a moment you "sent" yourself before you had a thought about it). Be in the moment, not in the past or the future. Remember you sent your Self this moment as a gift!

You keep changing
the boundaries.

ESSENTIAL TRUTH:

You have created your ideas of what is "right" and "wrong" simply to define Who You Are. Although you are nothing without these definitions, these boundaries, like me, you keep changing the boundaries as you change your ideas of Who You Are.

People's ideas of right and wrong change, and have changed over and over again from culture to culture, time period to time period, religion to religion, place to place . . . even from family to family and person to person. For example, burning a person at the stake for witchcraft was once considered "right," and today prostitution is "wrong" in one location, but not in another.

And so it is that there are no "rotten apples" in the barrel. There are only people who disagree with your point of view on things, people who construct a different model of the world from yours. We are all making up the rules as we go along, changing the boundaries to fit our Present Reality, reassessing Who We Are, and that's perfectly all right. In fact, it's as it should be, must be, if we are to be evolving beings.

Everything is occurring perfectly.

ESSENTIAL TRUTH:

Throughout history we have had remarkable teachers, each presenting extraordinary opportunities to remember Who We Really Are. These teachers have shown us the highest and the lowest of the human potential. They have presented vivid, breathtaking examples of what it can mean to be human.

Everything occurring in the universe (including death) is occurring perfectly. God hasn't made a mistake in a very long time! The secret of understanding this is knowing the purpose behind all events. All events, all experiences, have as their purpose the creating of opportunity. Events and experiences are opportunities. Nothing more, nothing less. They are things that happen and it is what we think of them, do about them, be in response to them, that gives them meaning.

Remember, these opportunities are drawn to you, created by you (both individually and collectively) as tools in the creation and experiencing of Who You Are. And Who You Are is a being of much higher consciousness than you are probably now exhibiting!

Consciousness
is everything.

ESSENTIAL TRUTH:

The inability of most people to experience the suffering of the masses, the oppression of minorities, the anger of the underclass, or the survival needs of anyone but themselves or their immediate families as one's own, is what allows such suffering to continue. Separation breeds indifference, false superiority. Unity produces compassion, genuine equality.

Group consciousness is something that is not widely understood—yet it is extremely powerful and can, if you are not careful, often overcome individual consciousness. So be aware of the effect that your group's consciousness can have on you, where it could lead you, and whether it reflects and matches your own.

Our world, and the condition it is in, is a reflection of the total, combined consciousness of everyone living on it. So unless we are satisfied with it the way it is, we can see there is much to be done. Individual consciousness and small groups can in turn affect larger groups and ultimately the largest group of all, which is ALL of humankind. Therefore, seek to find a group whose consciousness matches your own, or be the source of one, and others of like consciousness will be drawn to you.

Remember that consciousness is everything, and creates your experience. Group consciousness is powerful and produces outcomes of unspeakable beauty or ugliness. The choice is always yours. It begins with you.

There is no time.

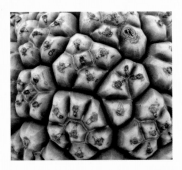

Essential Truth:

"Time" is not a continuum. It is an element of relativity that exists vertically, not horizontally. Don't think of it as a "left-to-right" thing—a so-called time line that runs from birth to death for each individual, and from some infinite point to some finite point for the universe. "Time" is an "up-and-down" thing. Think of it as a spindle, representing the Eternal Moment of Now. Now picture leaves of paper on the spindle, one atop the other. These are the elements of time. Each element separate and distinct, yet each existing simultaneously with the other. All the paper on the spindle at once! As much as there will ever be—as much as there ever was . . . All things exist simultaneously. All events occur at once.

And so, yesterday and tomorrow are figments of our imagination. Constructions of our minds, and nonexistent in Ultimate Reality. All that is required is for us to grasp that there is no time but this time. "Now" is all there is.

Einstein understood that it is not time which "passes," but objects which pass through, and move around in, a static field which you call space. "Time" is simply our way of counting movements!

A true understanding of time allows us to live much more peacefully with our reality of relativity, where time is experienced as a movement, a flow, rather than a constant. It is you who are moving, not time. Time has no movement. There is only One Moment.

You exist everywhere.

Essential Truth:

You must know—you are now ready to be told—that you exist at every level of the space-time continuum simultaneously. That is, your soul Always Was, Always Is, and Always Will Be—world without end—amen.

You exist everywhere and at all times. Even though "future" and "past" do not exist, you exist in more places than one. There is only one of you, but you are much larger than you think. You are a Divine Being of Divine Proportion with an evolving soul.

Your Divine Being is capable of more than one experience at the same "time"—and able to divide your Self into as many different "selves" as you choose. You can live the "same life" over and over again, in different ways, and you can also live different lives at different "times" on the continuum. Thus, all the while you're being you, here, now—you can also be, and have been, other "selves" in other "times" and "places."

Just know this: You are a being of Divine Proportion, knowing no limitation. A part of you is choosing to know yourself as your presently experienced Identity. Yet this is by far not the limit of your Being, although you think that it is. Why do you think this? Because you must think that it is, or you cannot do what you've given yourself this life to do.

Bless the process.

Essential Truth:

It would be very difficult for you to play this wonderful game of life if you had full awareness of what is going on. If you did, the "game" would be over! The Process depends on the Process being complete, as it is—including your lack of total awareness at this stage.

So, bless the Process, and accept it as the greatest gift of the Kindest Creator. Embrace the Process, and move through it with peace and wisdom and joy. Use the Process, and transform it from something you endure to something you engage as a tool in the creation of the most magnificent experience of All Time: the fulfillment of your Divine Self.

And how best do you do that?

By deciding Who You Are—Who You Want to Be—and then doing everything in your power to be that.

Space is time . . . demonstrated.

ESSENTIAL TRUTH:

In truth there is no such thing as space—pure "empty" space, with nothing in it. Everything is something. Even the "emptiest" space is filled with vapors so thin, so stretched out over infinite areas, that they seem to not be there. Then, after the vapors are gone, there is energy. Pure energy. This manifests as vibration. Oscillations. Movements of the All at a particular frequency. Invisible "energy" is the "space" which holds "matter together." Actually, what you now call matter is mostly space. All "solid" objects are 2 percent solid "matter" and 98 percent "air"! The space between the tiniest particles of matter in all objects is enormous. It is something like the distance between heavenly bodies in your night sky. Yet these objects you call solid. At one point the entire universe actually was "solid," and there was also a "time" before that "time" when there was no matter at all—just the purest form of Highest Vibration Energy, but this was the time "before" time—before the physical universe as you know it existed.

In the beginning, pure energy—Me!—vibrated, oscillated, so fast as to form matter—all the matter of the universe—in a process so-called the Big Bang. You, too, can perform the same feat. In fact, you do, every day. Your thoughts are pure vibration—and they can and do create physical matter!

Simply understand that all things are cyclical—including life itself. Understanding about the life of the universe will help you to understand about the life of the universe inside you, so you become more able to enjoy the Process—not merely endure it. There is a natural rhythm to life, and everything moves to that rhythm; everything goes with that flow. Thus it is written: "For everything there is a season; and a time for every Purpose under Heaven."

You cannot give what you do not have.

Essential Truth:

All of your life you have been taught that it is better to give than to receive. Yet you cannot give what you do not have. This is why self-gratification is so important—and why it is so unfortunate that it has come to sound so ugly.

Obviously, self-gratification at the expense of others is not what we're talking about here. This is not about ignoring the needs of others. Yet life should also not have to be about ignoring your own needs. It's about choosing all the good that life has to offer!

So go ahead and choose the adulation of others—but see all others as beings upon which you can shower adulation, and do it! Go ahead and choose being better—but not better than others; rather, better than you were before. Go ahead and choose having more, but only so that you have more to give. And yes, choose "knowing how" and "knowing why"—so that you can share all knowledge with others. And by all means choose to KNOW GOD. In fact, CHOOSE THIS FIRST, and all else will follow.

Give yourself abundant pleasure, and you will have abundant pleasure to give others.

Self-denial is
self-destruction.

ESSENTIAL TRUTH:

"Feeling good" is the soul's way of shouting, "This is who I am!" Doing what feels good is the road to heaven. I tell you this—no kind of evolution ever took place through denial. If you are to evolve, it will not be because you've been able to successfully deny yourself the things that you know "feel good," but because you've granted yourself those pleasures—and found something even greater.

Spirituality invites you to toss away the thoughts of others and come up with your own. "Feeling good" is your way of telling yourself that your last thought was truth, that your last word was wisdom, that your last action was love.

Self-denial is self-destruction, yet also know that self-regulation is not self-denial. Regulating one's behavior is an active choice to do or not to do something based on one's decision regarding who they are. If you are a person who respects the rights of others, then a decision not to cause hurt or disadvantage to another is hardly "self-denial." It is self-declaration. That is why it is said that the measure of how far one has evolved is what makes one feel good.

So grant yourself permission to have all that life has to offer.

All is the result of consciousness.

ESSENTIAL TRUTH:

I have built into all things an energy that transmits its signal throughout the universe. Every person, animal, plant, rock, tree—every physical thing—sends out energy, like a radio transmitter. You are sending off energy, emitting energy, right now from the center of your being in all directions. This energy, which is you, moves outward in wave patterns. The energy leaves you, moves through walls, over mountains, past the moon, and into Forever. It never, ever stops.

Every thought you've ever had colors this energy. Every word you've ever spoken shapes it. Everything you've ever done affects it. The vibration, the rate of speed, the wavelength, the frequency of your emanations, shift and change constantly with your thoughts, moods, feelings, words, and actions.

Now, every other person is naturally doing the same thing, and so the ether, the "air" between you, is filled with energy; a Matrix of intertwining, interwoven personal "vibes" that form a tapestry more complex than you could ever imagine. This weave is the combined energy field within which you live. It is powerful and affects everything, including you. You then send out newly created "vibes," impacted as you are by the incoming vibes to which you are being subjected, and these in turn add to and shift the Matrix—which in turn affects the energy field of everybody else, which impacts the vibes they send off, which impacts the Matrix—which impacts you . . . and so forth.

The Matrix—the combined current energy field—is a powerful vibe. It can directly impact, affect, and create physical objects and events. Your popular psychology has termed this energy Matrix the Collective Consciousness. It can and does affect everything on your planet—the prospects of war and the chances of peace; geophysical upheaval or a planet becalmed; widespread illness or worldwide wellness. And so it is that all is the result of consciousness.

You are emitting energy
in every direction.

ESSENTIAL TRUTH:

Your energy, beamed from you like a Golden Light, is interacting constantly with everything and everyone else. The closer you physically are, the more intense the energy. The farther away, the more subtle, yet you are never totally disconnected from any thing. Everyone and everything on the planet—and in the universe—is also emitting energy in every direction. This energy mixes with all other energies, crisscrossing in patterns of complexity beyond the ability of your most powerful computers to analyze.

The crisscrossing, intermingling, intertwining energies racing between everything that you can call physical is what holds physicality together. It is along this Matrix that you send signals to each other, messages, meanings, healings, and other physical effects—created sometimes by individuals but mostly by mass consciousness. These innumerable energies are attracted to each other, and this is called the Law of Attraction. In this Law, Like attracts Like.

Like thoughts attract Like thoughts along the Matrix, and when enough of these similar energies "clump together," so to speak, their vibrations become heavier, they slow down, and some become Matter. Thoughts do create physical form and when many people are thinking the same thing, there is a very high likelihood their thoughts will form a Reality. It is true therefore that both unified prayer and un-prayerlike thoughts can create "effects." A worldwide consciousness of fear, for instance, or anger, or lack, or insufficiency, can create that experience—across the globe or within a given locale where those collective ideas are strongest.

This dance . . . this energy interaction, is occurring all the time—in and with everything!

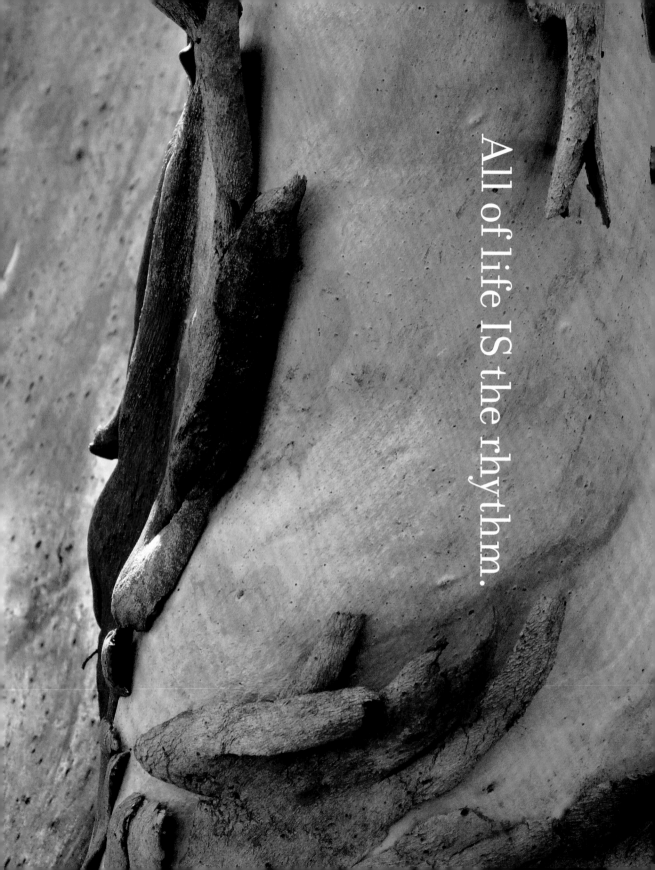

All of life IS the rhythm.

ESSENTIAL TRUTH:

The Matrix (the Law of Attraction) draws itself into itself exactly as your scientists describe the so-called Black Hole phenomenon. It pulls like-energy to like-energy, even drawing physical objects toward each other. Those objects must then repel each other, move away, or they will merge forever—in effect, disappearing in their present form and taking on a new form. All beings of consciousness intuitively know this, and so move away from the Permanent Melding in order to maintain their relationship to all other beings. If they did not, they would meld into all other beings and experience the Oneness Forever. This is the state from which we have come.

This ebb and flow, "to" and "fro" movement is the basic rhythm of the universe, and every thing in it. This is sex—the Synergistic Energy eXchange. You are constantly being attracted to one another and with all that is in the Matrix, although your choice is to remain free of the Unity, so that you can experience it.

Now, this natural rhythm of the universe typifies all of life—including the very movements that create life in your reality. All of life works on such a rhythm; all of life IS the rhythm—the gentle rhythm of God—the cycles of life. Food grows in such cycles. Seasons come and go. Planets spin and circle. Suns explode and implode, and the Universes breathe in and breathe out. All of it happens in cycles and in rhythms, in vibrations matching the frequencies of God.

It's time to make friends with your mind again.

ESSENTIAL TRUTH:

You are a three-part being and most people only experience themselves as a body. The mind is forgotten after age 30, it is not nourished, not expanded. Most people only do the minimum output required, so the mind is not fed, not awakened—it is lulled, dulled. So most people live life on a body level—feed the body, clothe the body, give the body "stuff." The truth is, most people don't want to have to think for themselves. "Make it easy for me. Tell me what to do, what are the rules, where are my boundaries? Tell me, tell me, somebody just tell me!" Then when things go wrong or turn sour they get disgusted, disillusioned, because they followed all the rules, they did as they were told, and then they ask: Why did it fall apart? What went wrong? Well, it fell apart the moment you abandoned your mind—the greatest creative tool you ever had.

It's time to make friends with your mind again. Be a companion to it, be a nourisher of it. Some of you, a small minority, have understood that you have a body and a mind and have treated your mind well, but few have learned to use the mind at more than one-tenth its capacity. If you knew what your mind is capable of, you would never cease to partake of its wonders and its powers.

And if you think the number of you who balance your life between your body and your mind is small, the number who see yourselves as three-part beings (Body, Mind, and Spirit) is minuscule.

When you live as a single-faceted creature, you become deeply immersed in matters of the body—physical stimulations and satisfactions. When you live as a dual-faceted creature, you broaden your concerns to include matters of the mind—companionship, creativity, stimulation of new thoughts, new ideas, creation of new goals, new challenges, personal growth.

You are an amazing three-part being. You are more than your body, and so much more than just a body with a mind.

When was the last time you
said hello to your soul?

ESSENTIAL TRUTH:

Are you nurturing your soul? Are you even noticing it? Are you healing it or hurting it? Are you growing or withering? Are you expanding or contracting? Is your soul as lonely as your mind? Is it even more neglected? And when was the last time you felt your soul being expressed?

When was the last time you cried with joy? Wrote poetry? Made music? Danced in the rain? Baked a pie? Painted anything? Fixed something that was broken? Kissed a baby? Held a cat to your face? Hiked up a hill? Swam naked? Walked at sunrise? Played the harmonica? Talked until dawn? Made love for hours . . . on a beach, in the woods? Communed with nature? Searched for God?

When was the last time you sat alone with the silence, traveling to the deepest part of your being? When was the last time you said hello to your soul? When you live as a three-part being . . . you come at last into balance with yourself. Your concerns include matters of the soul: spiritual identity; life purpose; relationship to God; path of evolution; spiritual growth; ultimate destiny.

As you evolve into higher and higher states of consciousness, you bring into full realization every aspect of your being: body, mind, and soul. Yet evolution does not mean dropping some aspects of Self in favor of others. It simply means expanding focus; turning away from exclusive involvement with one aspect, such as "the body," toward genuine love and appreciation of all aspects.

Enjoy everything. Need nothing.

ESSENTIAL TRUTH:

Is there such a thing as "too much" of something? The answer is: No. Of course not! But there is such a thing as too much of a need for something!

In our personal relationships, needing someone is the fastest way to kill the relationship. So, feel unneeded instead—for the greatest gift you can give someone is the strength and the power not to need you, to need you for nothing.

And so God suggests this:

Enjoy everything. Need nothing.

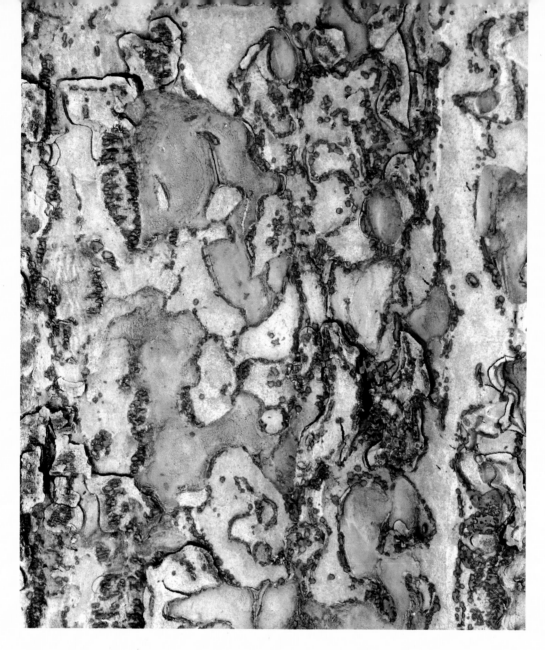

Education has very little
to do with knowledge.

154

ESSENTIAL TRUTH:

God has observed that most of us have misunderstood the meaning, the purpose, and the function of our children's education, to say nothing of the process by which it is best undertaken. We have decided that the meaning and the purpose and the function of education is to pass on knowledge; that to educate someone is to give them knowledge—that is, the accumulated knowledge of one's particular family, clan, tribe, society, nation, and world. Yet education has very little to do with knowledge. It has to do with Wisdom!

Wisdom is knowledge applied. And we are ignoring wisdom in favor of knowledge. We are teaching our children what to think instead of how to think. God explains that: When you give your children knowledge, you are telling them what to think. That is, you are telling them what they are supposed to know, what you want them to understand is true. When you give your children wisdom, you do not tell them what to know, or what is true, but, rather, how to get to their own truth! Yet you cannot ignore knowledge in favor of wisdom, because a certain amount of knowledge must be passed on from one generation to the next—obviously! But as little knowledge as possible—the smaller amount, the better.

Ideally, schools could have classes in critical thinking, problem solving, and logic instead of a system based on the development in the child of memories, not abilities. At the moment, children are taught to remember facts and fictions—the fictions each society has set up about itself. Programs that develop abilities and skills rather than memories are ridiculed by those who imagine that they know what a child needs to learn. History is supposed to be an accurate and full account of what really happened. Politics is always one's point of view about what happened. History, truly written, uncovers, tells all. Politics covers, tells, only one side, and so the mistakes of the past are justified and repeated. Your elders have set up a historical value system which says that "might is right" and created a world which solves problems with violence. Your children have not been taught differently. They have not been allowed to critically analyze what their elders have been doing, they have only been allowed to memorize it. Unfortunately, what you memorize, you memorialize.

Your world has run amok, because of what you have not allowed your education systems to teach. You have not allowed your schools to teach that love is all there is. You have not allowed your schools to speak of a love which is unconditional. You need to let the child discover for itself. Know this: Knowledge is lost. Wisdom is never forgotten.

Teach
your
children
the three
Core
Concepts
for living.

ESSENTIAL TRUTH:

Children remember everything they see, everything they experience. Why, then, do you place your children in schools where competition is allowed and encouraged, where being the "best" and learning the "most" is rewarded, where "performance" is graded, and where moving at one's own pace is barely tolerated? What does your child understand from this?

Instead, teach your children of movement and music and the joy of art, and the mystery of fairy tales and the wonder of life. Bring out what is naturally found in the child, rather than seek to put in what is unnatural to the child. Allow young ones to learn logic and critical thinking, and problem solving and creation, using the tools of their own intuition and their deepest inner knowing, rather than the rules and the memorized systems and conclusions of a society which has already proven itself to be wholly unable to evolve by these methods, yet continues to use them.

Teach concepts, not subjects, built around the three Core Concepts of Awareness, Honesty, and Responsibility, and teach them from the earliest age until the final day. Base your entire educational model upon them. These concepts along with many others must be deeply understood if children are to evolve and grow into complete human beings. They are the most important things in life. For example, teach what it means to be honest, to be responsible, to be aware of other people's feelings and respectful of other people's paths.

For thousands of years we have been making the same mistakes because we have been teaching the same things. We have not evolved. We need to look at our societies' values and restructure them, then take the grandest vision and teach it in our schools.

Truth and politics
do not mix.

ESSENTIAL TRUTH:

There are very few governments which do not deliberately mislead their people. Government is the perfect portrayer of the accuracy of the axiom that if you lie big enough, long enough, the lie becomes the "truth." Truth and politics do not and cannot mix because politics is the art of saying only what needs to be said and saying it in just the right way in order to achieve a desired end. Not all politics are bad, but the art of politics is a practical art. It recognizes with great candor the psychology of most people. It simply notices that most people operate out of self-interest. So politics is the way that people of power seek to convince you that their self-interest is your own, and governments understand self-interest. That is why they design programs which give things to people. When governments began to be the people's provider, as well as the people's protector, they started creating society, rather than preserving it.

When providing for people's needs, government must be careful not to rob the people of their greatest dignity: the exercise of personal power, individual creativity, and the single-minded ingenuity which allows people to notice that they can provide for themselves. A delicate balance must be struck. You cannot grow and become great when you are constantly being told what to do by government. More often than not, your laws are the announcements of what those in power think you should be, but are not. The "elitist few" instruct the "ignorant many" through the laws. You must take care not to smother yourself in laws—you cannot legislate morality, you cannot mandate equality. What is needed is a shift in collective consciousness, not an enforcer of collective conscience. Our behavior (and all laws and government programs) must spring from Beingness and must be a true reflection of Who We Are and want to be as a society.

Our laws reflect
where the power is.

Essential Truth:

In great societies very few laws are necessary, and although God is not suggesting a world with no codes of behavior or agreements, he does suggest they be based on a higher understanding and a grander definition of self-interest.

What most of our laws actually do say is what the most powerful among us have as their vested interest. For example, the real reason hemp is outlawed and tobacco is not has nothing to do with health. It has to do with economics, which is . . . power! If hemp were to be grown legally, half the cotton growers, nylon and rayon manufacturers, and timber products people in the world would go out of business. It is the same reason you have taken so long to mass-produce electric cars, provide affordable, sensible health care, or use solar heat and solar power in every home, even though you've had the technology to produce all these things for years. To find the answer, look to see who would lose money if you did.

Whenever the common good or collective good is mentioned, everyone yells, "Communism!" In your society, if providing for the good of the many does not produce a huge profit for someone, the good of the many is more often than not ignored. The basic question facing humankind, therefore, is: Can self-interest ever be replaced by the best interests, the common interest, of humankind?

You must decide whether
you simply care for each other.

ESSENTIAL TRUTH:

So long as no one sees another's plight as his own, the daily atrocities suffered by the under-privileged everywhere will not alter the attitudes of our wasteful, decadent society. It is also a sad observation that these attitudes that sicken the heart are epidemic around the world. No one seems to have the power to alter these conditions, yet the truth is, power is not the problem. No one seems to have the will, because you do not care. It is a lack of caring. The entire planet faces a crisis of consciousness. You must decide whether you simply care for each other.

You do love the members of your own family. You simply have a very limited view of who your family members are. You do not consider yourself part of the human family, and so the problems of the human family are not your own. We need to construct a new model of the world by eliminating all separations between the world's people. Presently, we see the world as a collection, a group, of nation-states, each sovereign, separate, and independent of each other. Unless and until one affects the group as a whole (or the most powerful members of that group), no one cares. Thousands could starve, for instance, and no one would much care, calling it an "internal problem." But when your interests are threatened there, when your investments, your security, your quality of life are affected, you rush in where angels fear to tread. You then tell the Big Lie: it is for humanitarian reasons. The proof of this is that where you do not have interests, you do not have concern.

For the world to change, you must begin to see someone else's interests as your own.

The only problem of
humanity is lack of love.

ESSENTIAL TRUTH:

It is time for the world to stop kidding itself, to wake up, to realize that the only problem of humanity is lack of love. Love breeds tolerance, tolerance breeds peace. Intolerance produces war and looks indifferently upon intolerable conditions. Love cannot be indifferent. It does not know how. The fastest way to get to a place of love and concern for all humankind is to see all humankind as your family. The fastest way to see all humankind as your family is to stop separating yourself.

If we were to choose to have a new relationship between all the people and nations on our planet—to choose to get to a place of love and concern for all humankind—we would need to form a new world political community. A community where each nation-state had an equal say in the world's affairs, and an equal proportionate share of the world's resources. The result would be in the best interests of everyone, because billions of dollars a year would be added to the global economies—dollars which could be spent to feed the hungry, clothe the needy, house the poor, bring security to the elderly, provide better health, and produce a dignified standard of living for all. The causes of crime would be lost . . . new jobs would mushroom . . . and all of these benefits would result from the simple restructuring of your worldview—the simpler reordering of your world political configuration.

If each of the nation-states in the world today were to join together in a United Federation, the people of the world would have greater security and safety, and great prosperity, too, by cooperating with, rather than fighting with, each other.

There is nothing in this world that could not be overcome if every decision was made in answer to this one simple question: What would love do now?

SPIRITUAL
truth must be *lived*.

ESSENTIAL TRUTH:

So long as humans remain attached to outer things, there will be disagreements and war. However, there is a way to truly eliminate war—and all experience of unrest and lack of peace—but it is a spiritual solution, and spiritual truth must be lived in practical life to change everyday experience.

So until that consciousness is possible, the trick would be to combine both a new global political and spiritual solution into one, until a wider spiritual change can occur. There would still be disagreements, yet there need not be wars and there need not be killing. If the world could come together to create a system for the resolution of the differences, one that eliminates the need for war (and even the possibility of it), it would, quite simply, improve the quality of life for all people—the everyday experience of all people.

The struggles of the world cannot be solved from an Outside World consciousness, but only from living within a spiritual consciousness.

All conflict arises from misplaced desire.

ESSENTIAL TRUTH:

Ultimately, every global political problem, just as every personal problem, breaks down to a spiritual problem. All of life is spiritual, and therefore all of life's problems are spiritually based, and spiritually solved.

Wars are created on your planet because somebody has something that somebody else wants. This is what causes someone to do something that somebody else does not want them to do. All conflict arises from misplaced desire. The only peace in all the world that is sustaining is Internal Peace.

When you find peace within, you also find that you can do without, which simply means that you no longer need the things in your Outside World. "Not needing" is a great freedom, that frees you firstly from fear: fear that there is something you won't have; fear that there is something you have that you will lose; or fear that without a certain thing you won't be happy.

"Not needing" frees you from anger. If you derive your life's greatest happiness from the desire of experiences obtainable only in the Outside World—the physical world outside of yourself—you will not find peace.

TRAGEDY

In a moment of great tragedy,
the challenge always is to
quiet the mind and
move deep within
the soul.

"Fear not, for I am with you."
That is what poetry has to say to the person facing tragedy.

In your darkest hour, I will be your light.
In your blackest moment, I will be your consolation.
In your most difficult and trying time, I will be your strength.
Therefore, have faith!

For I am your shepherd; you shall not want.

I will cause you to lie down in green pastures;

I will lead you beside still waters.
I will restore your soul, and lead you in the paths of
righteousness for My Name's sake.

And yea, though you walk through the valley of the
Shadow of Death; you will fear no evil; for I am with you.
My rod and My staff will comfort you.

I am preparing a table before you in the presence
of your enemies.

I shall anoint your head with oil.
Your cup will run over.

Surely, goodness and mercy will follow you all
the days of your life, and you will dwell in
My house—in My heart—forever.

Anger is fear announced.

ESSENTIAL TRUTH:

When you have nothing to fear, you have nothing over which to be angry. "Not needing" something frees you from anger.

You are not angry when you don't get what you want, because your wanting it was simply a preference, not a necessity. You therefore have no fear associated with the possibility of not getting it. Hence, no anger.

You are not angry when you see others doing what you don't want them to do, because you don't need them to do or not do any particular thing. Hence no anger. You are not angry when someone is unkind, because you have no need for them to be kind. You have no anger when someone is unloving, because you have no need for them to love you. You have no anger when someone is cruel, or hurtful, or seeks to damage you, for you have no need for them to behave any other way, and you are clear you cannot be damaged. You do not even have anger should someone seek to take your life, because you do not fear death.

When fear is taken from you, all else can be taken from you and you will not be angry. You know inwardly, intuitively, that every thing you've created can be created again, or—more importantly—that it doesn't matter.

When you find Inner Peace, neither the presence nor the absence of any person, place or thing, condition, circumstance, or situation can be the Creator of your state of mind or the cause of your experience of being. You can then experience being fully in your body and the delights of that.

Strive to see the perfection
in everything.

Essential Truth:

When we are hungry or without shelter, when our loved ones are dying, or we are under attack or being violated—it is difficult to hear that there is perfection in everything. In other words, when we are in the midst of the greatest tragedy, God asks us to see the glory of the process, to strive to see the perfection. It is a change in consciousness that He is speaking about, and you don't have to do this, of course. It depends on how you wish to experience the moment. But Gods tells us that in the moment of great tragedy the challenge always is to quiet the mind and move deep within the soul. In fact, you automatically do this when you have no control over it.

Now, this sounds like such an impossible thing to do—to need nothing, desire every thing, and choose what shows up! Yet when you move to God consciousness, you can do it. If you talk with a person who has faced a near-death accident or horrific event, they often will tell you that time slowed way down, that they were overcome by a curious calm, that there was no fear at all.

God says, "Fear not, for I am with you. . . . In your most difficult and trying time, I will be your light, your consolation, your strength. Therefore, have faith, for I am your Shepherd!"

The Game of Life

I have devised a way for you to create
anew, and Know, Who You Are
in your experience.

I did this by providing you with:

1. **Relativity**—a system wherein you could exist as a thing in relationship to something else.
2. **Forgetfulness**—a process by which you willingly submit to total amnesia, so that you can not know that relativity is merely a trick, and that you are All of it.
3. **Consciousness**—a state of being in which you grow until you reach full awareness, then become a True and Living God, creating and experiencing your own reality, expanding and exploring that reality, changing and re-creating that reality as you stretch your consciousness to new limits—or, shall we say, to no limit.

In this paradigm, Consciousness is everything. Consciousness—that of which you are truly aware—is the basis of all truth and thus of all true spirituality.

And what is the point of all this? It is so that you can create Who You Are and Who You Want to Be. This is the act of God being God. It is Me being Me—through you!

This is the point of all life.

There is only one question
of any relevance.

ESSENTIAL TRUTH:

The attitude held by many people is that the poor have been given enough; and the poor are poor basically because they want to be or deserve to be. People cite "from each according to his ability, to each according to his need" as evidence of the idea of ensuring the basic human dignity of all, through the efforts of everyone. They also hold steadfastly to "every man for himself."

However, God asks whether these thoughts serve you. When looking at the world, that is the question people have to ask themselves. Does it serve you to hold those thoughts? In other words, in terms of Who You Are and Who You Seek to Be, do those thoughts serve you?

It is true that there are many people in this world who are observably disadvantaged, indeed, entire groups of people. And it may also be true that the soul may wish to work with a handicapped body or experience a repressive society in this lifetime, in order to produce the conditions needed to accomplish what it has set out to do. However, remember first that everything you think, say, and do is a reflection of what you've decided about yourself; a statement of Who You Are; an act of creation in your deciding Who You Want to Be. Therefore, in every circumstance as you encounter life, ask yourself this question: Who am I and who do I choose to be, in relationship to this?

So, when you next see a person who faces adversity or who appears not to have "made it" according to most, will it serve you to question whether "it's his own damn fault," as a statement to the universe of Who You Have Become?

No one is disadvantaged.

ESSENTIAL TRUTH:

It is true that at a very high metaphysical level, no one is "disadvantaged," for each soul creates for itself the exact people, events, and circumstances needed to accomplish what it wishes to accomplish. You choose everything. Your parents, your country of birth—all the circumstances surrounding your reentry, such as rebirth into a society under enormous political upheaval or with one with economic constraints, or the challenges of a diseased or physically handicapped body.

And throughout your life you continue to choose and to create people, events, and circumstances designed to bring you the exact, right, and perfect opportunities you now desire in order to know yourself as you truly are. In other words, no one is "disadvantaged," given what the soul wishes to accomplish, even though we see that people do face "disadvantages" in the physical sense. But these are actually the right and perfect conditions metaphysically.

Now, you are seeking to be and to experience Who You Really Are, and so within that context, when you come across a person who appears (in relative terms as observed in your world) to be less fortunate, the first question should always be: What do I want here? Did you hear that? Your first question, always, must be: What do I want here? Not: What does the other person want here? You do this so you can create Who You Are and Who You Want to Be. Do you want to be helpful, do you want to be loving, do you want to be and experience compassion and caring? Then look to see how you can best be those things. For this is the act of God being God.

Our nations play
the game of
"I'll Trade You."

ESSENTIAL TRUTH:

The game of "I'll Trade You" means, "You meet my needs and I'll meet yours."

Yet the purpose of all human relationships—relationships between nations as well as relationships between individuals—has nothing to do with any of this.

The purpose of your Holy Relationship with every other person, place, or thing is not to figure out what they want or need, but what you require or desire now in order to grow; in order to be Who You Want to Be.

What is needed on our planet is for our race to evolve to the point where we all do what is naturally right, not because of what we will gain from it, what we can "trade" you for it, or simply because you have something that we want. The game of "I'll trade you" would not exist if people everywhere simply traded in goodness and fairness—if everyone simply followed the Law of Love.

If every person on the planet had their basic needs met, if the mass of the people could live in dignity and escape the struggle of simple survival, then individual and universal glory, and greatness, would be achieved.

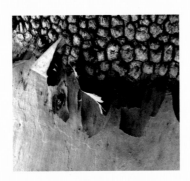

I Have Sent You
Nothing but Angels

To solve the problems that plague humankind,
we need a shift in consciousness and
that change can only be
made in the hearts of men.
We must stop seeing God as separate from us,
and us as separate from each other.
This is the future hope of our race and for our planet.
So how do we begin?

"By your shining example. Seek only Godliness. Speak only in truthfulness. Act only in love. Live the Law of Love now and forevermore. Give everything, require nothing. Avoid the mundane. Do not accept the unacceptable. Teach all who seek to learn of Me. Make every moment of your life an outpouring of love. Use every moment to think the highest thought, say the highest word, do the highest deed. In this, glorify your Holy Self, and thus, too, glorify Me. Bring peace to the Earth by bringing peace to all those whose lives you touch. Be peace. Feel and express in every moment your Divine Connection with the All, and with every person, place, and thing.

Embrace every circumstance, own every fault, share every joy, contemplate every mystery, walk in every man's shoes, forgive every offense (including your own), heal every heart, honor every person's truth, adore every person's God, protect every person's rights, preserve every person's dignity, promote every person's interests, provide every person's needs, presume every person's holiness, present every person's greatest gifts, produce every person's blessings, and pronounce every person's future secure in the assured love of God.

Be a living, breathing example of the Highest Truth that resides within you. Speak humbly of yourself lest someone mistake your Highest Truth for a boast. Speak softly, lest someone think you are merely calling for attention. Speak gently, that all might know of Love. Speak openly, lest anyone think you have something to hide. Speak candidly, so you cannot be mistaken. Speak often, so that your word may truly go forth. Speak respectfully, that no one be dishonored. Speak lovingly, that every syllable may heal. Speak of Me with every utterance.

Make of your life a gift. Remember always, you are the gift! Be a gift to everyone who enters your life, and to everyone whose life you enter. Be careful not to enter another's life if you cannot be a gift. (You can always be a gift, because you always are the gift—yet sometimes you don't let yourself know that.) When someone enters your life unexpectedly, look for the gift that person has come to receive from you.

When you see this simple truth, when you understand it, you see the greatest truth of all: I have sent you nothing but Angels!"

The greatest help
you can give another
person is to wake them up.

ESSENTIAL TRUTH:

Sometimes the best way to love someone, and the most help you can give, is to leave them alone or empower them to help themselves. It is like a feast. Life is a smorgasbord and you can give them a big helping of themselves. Remember that the greatest help you can give a person is to wake them up, to remind them of Who They Really Are.

There are many ways to do this. Sometimes with a little bit of help . . . a push, a shove, a nudge . . . and sometimes with a decision to let them run their course, follow their path, walk their walk, without any interference or intervention from you. What you have the opportunity to do is to re-mind them. That is, cause them to be of a New Mind about themselves. And you also have to be of a New Mind about them, for if you see them as unfortunate, they will be. Give people the help they ask for, rather than the help you want to give them, so as to empower them at the level at which they are ready to receive empowerment. However, make sure your help is offered in such a way that it creates continued independence, rather than dependence or reliance on you.

Then you will really be doing your best to help another.

Goodness and
fairness are
moral issues,
not political issues.

ESSENTIAL TRUTH:

Government is the human attempt to mandate goodness and ensure fairness. Yet there is only one place where goodness is born, and that is in the human heart. There is only one place where fairness can be conceptualized truly, and that is in the human mind. There is only one place where love can be experienced truly, and that is in the human soul. Because the human soul is love.

You cannot legislate morality. You cannot pass a law saying, "Love each other." Sharing must be a way of life, not an edict imposed by government. Sharing should be voluntary, not forced. Even basic laws—prohibitions against murdering, damaging, cheating, or even running a red light—shouldn't be needed and wouldn't be needed if all people everywhere simply followed the Laws of Love. In nonprimitive societies such laws are unnecessary, because all beings regulate themselves.

What is needed in our society is a growth in consciousness, not a growth of government, because goodness and fairness are moral issues, not political ones.

The evolution of a society is measured
by how well it treats the least
among its members.

ESSENTIAL TRUTH:

If God has placed more than sufficient resources on our planet to ensure adequate supplies for all—how can it be that so many starve to death, go homeless, and cry out for simple dignity? Isn't basic human dignity the birthright of everyone? Oughtn't it be? Must universal dignity be sacrificed to individual glory? And what kind of glory is obtained when it is achieved at the expense of another?

If the well-off say they do not want to help the starving and the homeless because they do not want to disempower them, then the well-off are hypocrites. For no one is truly "well-off" if they are well off while others are dying. If every person on the planet had basic needs met—if the mass of the people could live in dignity and escape the struggle of simple survival—would this not open the way for all of humankind to engage in more noble pursuits? If individual survival were guaranteed, then individual greatness could be achieved.

The evolution of a society is measured by how well it treats the least among its members. The challenge is to find the balance between helping people and hurting them. Are your fellow humans enlarged or reduced as a result of your help? Have you made them bigger or smaller? More able or less able? The challenge is not to make everyone equal, but to give everyone at least the assurance of basic survival with dignity, so that each may have the chance to choose what more they want from there.

Offer the help that is wanted.

ESSENTIAL TRUTH:

Never offer the kind of help that disempowers another. Never insist on offering the help you think is needed. Let the person or people in need know all that you have to give—then listen to what they want; see what they are ready to receive.

Offer the help that is wanted. Often, the person, or people, will say, or exhibit by their behavior, that they just want to be left alone. Despite what you think you'd like to give, leaving them alone might be the Highest Gift you can then offer. If, at a later time, something else is wanted or desired, you will be caused to notice if it is yours to give. If it is, then give it. Yet strive to give nothing which disempowers. That promotes or produces dependency and, in truth, there is always some way you can help others which also empowers them.

Completely ignoring the plight of another who is truly seeking your help is not the answer, for doing too little no more empowers the other than doing too much. To be of higher consciousness, you may not deliberately ignore the genuine plight of brothers or sisters, claiming that to let them "stew in their own juice" is the highest gift you can give them. That attitude is righteousness and arrogance at the highest level. It merely allows you to justify your noninvolvement.

Remember the teachings of Jesus: Verily, verily, I say unto you—inasmuch as you have done it to the least of these, My brethren, so have you done it to Me.

In other words: What you do to another, you do to yourself, because We Are All One.

Visibility is another name for truth.

ESSENTIAL TRUTH:

If the chief aim and goal of your society is the survival of all; the benefit, equality, of all; the providing of a good life for all; then your need for secrecy and quiet dealings and under-the-table maneuverings and money which can be hidden would disappear. Can you imagine what the people of money and power in the world would do if they thought that every move, every purchase, every sale, every dealing, every corporate action and pricing choice and wage negotiation, every decision could be reviewed by anyone? I tell you this: nothing breeds fairness faster than visibility. In enlightened societies there are no secrets, because no one is willing to get anything, or have anything, at someone else's expense.

The concept of visibility should also extend beyond monetary affairs and into all relationships; however, as a rule it doesn't, because most people still have too much to hide. In personal relationships (and in all relationships, really) it's about loss. It's about being afraid of what one might lose or fail to gain. Yet the best relationships, and certainly the best romantic ones, are relationships in which everyone knows everything; in which visibility is the only word; in which there simply are no secrets.

In these relationships nothing is withheld, nothing is shaded or colored or hidden or disguised. Nothing is left out or unspoken. There is no guesswork, or game-playing. And yet, visibility is not about having no mental privacy, no safe space in which to move through your personal process. What I'm talking about here is simply: being open and honest in your dealings with another; telling the truth when you speak. It's about telling it like it is. It's about fairness and openness and, well . . . visibility—simply another word for truth!

No one's point of view is less worthy of being heard than another's.

Essential Truth:

There have been great leaders who have been insightful enough and brave enough to propose the beginnings of new social structures in the modern world, in an attempt to find a solution to its political and social injustices. Sadly, mostly their efforts have been in vain. History will judge these men and women of wisdom, compassion, and courage as having personal visions that were miles ahead of their people.

These leaders came together in agreements that pulled the world back from violent confrontation time and time again, through the simple assertion of a simple truth: no one's point of view is less worthy of being heard than another's—no one human being has less dignity than another. It is interesting to note that these courageous leaders, each of whom brought the world from the brink of war in their own time, and each of whom espoused and proposed massive movements away from the prevailing political structure, each served only one term in office—removed by the very people they were seeking to elevate.

The solution to having a society of fairness and dignity for all, where everyone's point of view is considered just as worthy as another's, is, however, not a political one. The only real solution is a New Awareness and a New Consciousness.

An awareness of Oneness and a consciousness of Love.

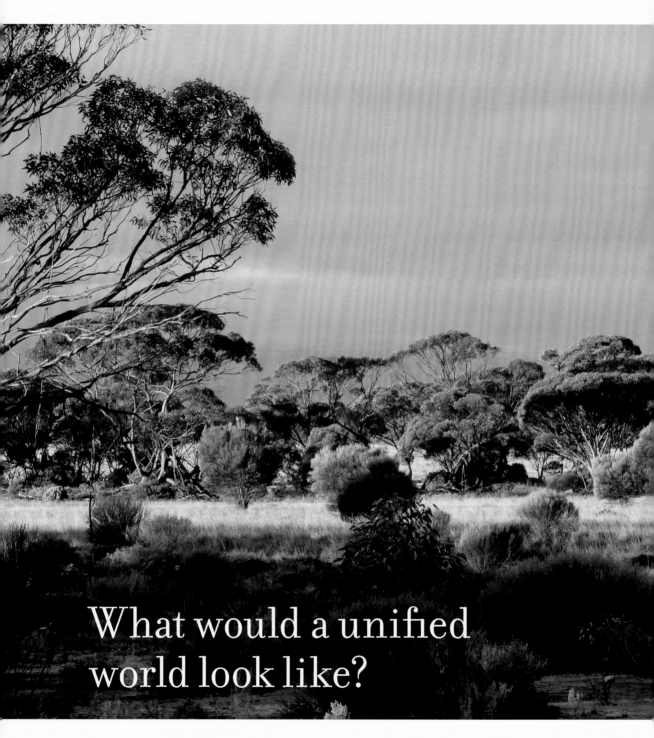

What would a unified world look like?

IT WOULD ACHIEVE:

1. An end to wars between nations and to the settling of disputes by killing.
2. An end to abject poverty, death by starvation, and mass exploitation of people and resources by those of power.
3. An end to the systematic environmental destruction of the Earth.
4. An escape from the endless struggle for bigger, better, more.
5. An opportunity—truly equal—for all people to rise to the highest expression of Self.
6. An end to all limitations and discriminations holding people back—whether in housing, in the workplace, in the political system, or in personal sexual relationships.

AND IT WOULD PRODUCE AN ENVIRONMENT WHERE:

All people would be offered a proper education. All people would be offered open opportunity to use that education in the workplace—to follow careers which bring them joy.

All people would be guaranteed access to health care whenever and however needed.

All people would be guaranteed they won't starve to death or have to live without sufficient clothing or adequate shelter.

All people would be granted the basic dignities of life so that survival would never again be the issue, so that simple comforts and basic dignities were provided all human beings.

TRY TO WRAP YOURSELF AROUND THIS THOUGHT:

People have a right to basic survival. Even if they do nothing. Even if they contribute nothing. Survival with dignity is one of the basic rights of life. I have given you enough resources to be able to guarantee that to everyone. All you have to do is share.

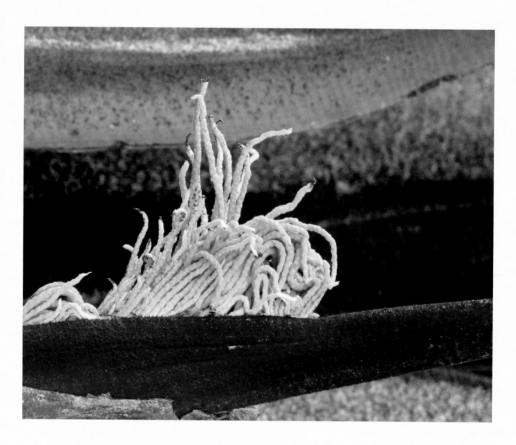

What makes a "better life"?

ESSENTIAL TRUTH:

"Living a better life" is a proper incentive. Creating a "better life" for your children is a good incentive. But the question is, what makes for a "better life"? How do you define "better"? How do you define "life"?

If you define "better" as bigger, better, more money, power, sex, and stuff . . . and if you define "life" as the period elapsing between birth and death in this your present existence, then you're doing nothing to get out of the trap that has created your planet's predicament. Yet if you define "better" as a larger experience and a greater expression of your grandest State of Being, and "life" as an eternal, ongoing, never-ending process of Being, you may yet find your way.

A "better life" is not created by the accumulation of things, and most of you know this, all of you say you understand it, yet your lives and the decisions you make which drive your lives have as much to do with "things" as anything else, and usually more. You strive for things, you work for things, and when you get some of the things you want, you never let them go.

It is because most of humankind believes that the obtainment and retainment of things creates a better life that enormous portions of the population are still struggling for simple physical survival. Such moral obscenities are only commonplace in a primitive society, where the purpose of life is misunderstood and the necessary shift is yet to be made toward what truly constitutes a "better life" for all the people of the world.

See life as a
spiritual encounter.

ESSENTIAL TRUTH:

The number of people on our planet who see life as a spiritual encounter is small. The greatest number of people in the world are only concerned with holding on to all that they have acquired and increasing their holdings. There is also another group, the smallest group of all, in fact, that has detached itself from the need for material things. They are concerned instead with spiritual truth, spiritual reality, and spiritual experience. The people in this group clearly see life as a spiritual encounter—a journey of the soul. They respond to all human events within that context. They hold all human experience within that paradigm.

Their struggle is not to achieve, acquire, obtain things. Their struggle has to do with the search for God, the fulfillment of Self, the expression of truth. As they evolve, this struggle becomes not a struggle at all, but a process. It is the process of Self-definition (not Self-discovery), of Growth (not learning), of Being (not doing).

The reason for seeking, striving, searching, stretching, and succeeding becomes completely different than that of other people. The reason for doing anything is changed, and with it the doer is likewise changed. The reason becomes the process, the doer becomes a be-er. Becomes what God created you to be—the physical out-picturing of Deity Itself.

What we need is equal *opportunity*, not *equality*.

ESSENTIAL TRUTH:

The people of the world do not need "equality" and we should be grateful for that. Because equality is sameness—and the last thing the world needs is sameness, or a world of automation where everything is identical. In fact, the richness of this world is in its contrasts.

What the people of the world do need is opportunity—equal opportunity. The opportunity—truly equal, for all people—to have access to education, health care, sufficient food, clothing, and shelter, and the basic dignities of life. Opportunity so that survival would never again be an issue. Opportunity so exploitation, limitation, and discrimination would no longer be possible.

And the opportunity—truly equal, for all people—to rise to the highest expression of Self—the equal opportunity for everyone to acquire knowledge, develop skills, and use these natural talents in the workplace.

And yet we see that, with all our world's resources and abundance, we have not yet managed to achieve these simple things, even though we think that as a society we are so advanced.

You cannot earn your way
into God's good graces.

ESSENTIAL TRUTH:

Your thought that the basic needs of survival and dignities of life need to be earned is the basis for your thought that you have to earn your way to heaven. Yet you cannot earn your way into God's good graces, and you do not have to, because you are already there. This is something you cannot accept, because it is something you cannot give. When you learn to give unconditionally (which is to say, love unconditionally), then will you learn to receive unconditionally.

This life was created as a vehicle through which you might be allowed to experience that. Even if people do nothing, contribute nothing, survival with dignity is one of the basic rights of life. I have given you enough resources to be able to guarantee that to everyone. All you have to do is share.

It is not for you to judge the journey of another's soul. It is for you to decide who you are, not who another has been or has failed to be. And so, when you ask what is wrong with people who simply waste their lives, lollygagging around, collecting "benefits"—the answer is: nothing. Because I observe that they are simply missing the greatest opportunity and the grandest glory: the opportunity to create and the glory of experiencing the highest idea of Who They Really Are.

The human spirit rises,

in the face of true

opportunity.

ESSENTIAL TRUTH:

In a world of true opportunity, where resources and abundance are shared, there may still be the "rich" and the "poor," but there would no longer be the "starving" and the "destitute." In other words, the incentives would not be taken out of life—merely the desperation. And what is it that would enable this paradigm to work—it would be the greatness of the human spirit.

Contrary to most people's belief, in the face of true opportunity, the average person would not be satisfied with subsistence levels and nothing more. In addition, the whole incentive for greatness would change if a spiritual shift took place.

With a shift away from material survival, there would be no other reason to achieve, to stand out, to become magnificent, save the experience of magnificence itself!

The human spirit rises, it does not fall, in the face of true opportunity. The soul seeks a higher experience of itself, not a lower one. Anyone who has experienced true magnificence, if only for a moment, knows this.

Conspiracy of silence.

It is the rich and powerful who support the social structures that keep the rich rich and the poor poor, and who staunchly resist any real effort to change the "system." They stand against any political or economic approach which seeks to provide true opportunity and genuine dignity to all people, even though most of the rich and powerful, taken individually, are certainly nice enough people, with as much compassion and sympathy as anyone.

Yet, what about the right of all people to live in minimally decent surroundings, with enough food to keep from starving, enough clothing to stay warm? What about the right of people everywhere to have adequate health care—the right not to have to suffer or die from relatively minor medical complications which those with money overcome with the snap of a finger?

The resources of our planet—including the fruits of the labors of the masses of the indescribably poor who are continually and systematically exploited—belong to all the world's people, not just those who are rich and powerful enough to do the exploiting. This system of exploitation can exist only in a world motivated by greed, where profit margin, not human dignity, is the first consideration.

So the conspiracy system continues, and for most of the rich and powerful it is not a conspiracy of action, but a conspiracy of silence. We do nothing about the obscenity of this socioeconomic system, other than to tell everyone how proud we all are of our world's Free Market Economy.

Yet it is written:

If thou wilt be perfect,
go and sell what thou hast, and give to the poor,
and thou shalt have treasure in heaven.
But when the young man heard this,
he went away, sorrowful,
for he had great possessions.

211

Joy at the workplace
has nothing to do
with function.

ESSENTIAL TRUTH:

One day our society will shift to a consciousness where a new workplace system will allow all people the opportunity of providing more than the basic necessities and comforts of life for themselves and their families. It will allow the conditions within which every person can accumulate abundance to the level that they wish. With the struggle of simple survival eliminated and the basic needs of everyone met, a new level of dignity and purpose would arise.

True opportunity in the workplace would bring satisfaction and joy, if the option to work was chosen by an individual. However, in this consciousness, not everyone would choose to "work." There would be those who would see their life activity as real work and would choose to stop "working" outside of this. And there would be those who would see their work activity as absolute joy, who would never stop.

In this consciousness, everyone could have a job in the "Joy Place," for when a society allows for everyone to have equal opportunity, everyone can acquire knowledge, develop skills, and use their natural talents in the Joy Place—the "workplace."

Because joy at the workplace has nothing to do with function, and everything to do with purpose.

The mother who wakes up at 4 o'clock in the morning to change her baby's diaper understands this perfectly. She hums and coos to the baby, and for all the world it doesn't look like what she is doing is any work at all. Yet it is her attitude about what she is doing, it is her intention with regard to it, it is her purpose in undertaking this activity, which make the activity a true joy.

The highest purpose of life is . . .
the doing of the greatest good.

ESSENTIAL TRUTH:

From the beginning, God has given you the freedom to create your life, and hence your Self, as you wish to be. You cannot know your Self as the Creator if He tells you what to create, how to create, and then forces, requires, or causes you to do so. Otherwise His purpose is lost.

God has told us that our economic, political, social, and religious systems are primitive. And yet, He observes that we have the collective arrogance to think they are the best. He sees the largest number of us resisting any change or improvement which takes anything away from ourselves—never mind who it might help.

God tells us that what is needed on our planet is a massive shift in consciousness. A change in our awareness. A renewed respect for all of life, and a deepened understanding of the interrelatedness of everything. What we need is a consciousness shift, an awareness that the highest purpose of life is not the accumulation of the greatest wealth, but the doing of the greatest good—and a corollary awareness that, indeed, the concentration of wealth, not the sharing of the wealth, is the largest factor in the creation of the world's most persistent and striking social and political dilemmas.

This single factor ensures that the masses of people remain regulated, controlled, and subservient.

True law is natural law.

ESSENTIAL TRUTH:

Truth—like natural law—is observable. It is self-evident and therefore does not have to be explained to you. Any law that is not natural law is not observable, so it has to be explained to you, shown to you; you need to be told why it's for your own good.

This is not an easy task because if a thing is for your own good, it is self-evident. Only that which is not self-evident has to be explained to you. For example, scientists aren't very talkative—they conduct an experiment and simply show you what they've done—the results speak for themselves, so verbosity is not necessary. Not so with politicians. Even if they failed, they talk. The same for religious leaders—the more they fail, the more they talk.

Yet I tell you this—Truth and God are found in the same place: in the silence. When you have found God and when you have found truth, it is not necessary to talk about it. It is self-evident.

True law is natural law—inexplicable and not needed to be explained or taught. It is observable. True law is that law by which the people freely agree to be governed because they are governed by it naturally. Their agreement is therefore not so much an agreement as it is a mutual recognition of what is So. Those laws don't have to be enforced. They already are enforced, by the simple expedient of undeniable consequence.

For example, Highly Evolved Beings do not hit themselves on the head with a hammer, because it hurts; nor do they hit another, for the same reason. They have noticed that with this behavior, sooner or later you're going to get hurt. This result is observable, but when primitive beings observe the same thing—they simply don't care about the consequences. A primitive race is one where strength is all they understand. Evolved beings are not willing to play this game, whereas primitive beings play nothing else. It is therefore observable that there is no true law on our planet.

Abandon the concept
of separation.

ESSENTIAL TRUTH:

Most, if not all, of the world's problems and conflicts, and of your problems and conflicts as individuals, would be solved and resolved if you would, as a society:

(1) Abandon the concept of Separation; and (2) adopt the concept of Visibility.

Never see yourself again as separate from one another, or from Me. Never tell anything but the whole truth to anyone, or accept anything less than your grandest truth about Me. The first choice will produce the second, for when you understand that you are One with Everyone, you cannot tell an untruth or withhold important data or be anything but totally visible with all others, because you will be clear that it is in your own best interests to do so.

This will take great wisdom, courage, and determination, for Fear will make these magnificent truths appear hollow and will distort, disdain, destroy them. Fear will be your greatest enemy, but you cannot produce the society you have yearned and dreamed of until you see with clarity the ultimate truth: that what you do to others, you do to yourself; what you fail to do for others, you fail to do for yourself; that the pain of others is your pain and the joy of others your joy; and that when you disclaim any part of it, you disclaim a part of yourself. We are always united, you and I. We cannot not be. It is simply impossible. Remember, then, that you are now simply living in the unconscious experience of that unification—in the illusion of separation.

Now is the time
to reclaim yourself.

ESSENTIAL TRUTH:

Now is the time to reclaim yourself.

Now is the time to see yourself as Who You Really Are, and thus render yourself visible again—to adopt the concept of Visibility. For when you and your true relationship with God become visible, then We are indivisible. And nothing will ever divide Us again.

And although you will live again in the illusion of separation, using it as a tool to create your Self anew, you will henceforth move through your incarnations with enlightenment, seeing the illusion for what it is, using it playfully and joyfully to experience any aspect of Who You Are which it pleases you to experience, yet nevermore accepting it as reality. You will nevermore have to use the device of forgetfulness in order to re-create your Self anew, but will use Separation knowingly, simply choosing to manifest as That Which Is Separate for a particular reason and a particular purpose.

And when you are thus totally enlightened—that is, once more filled with the light—you may even choose, as your particular reason for returning to physical life, the re-minding of others. You may select to return to this physical life not to create and experience any new aspect of your Self, but to bring the light of truth to this place of illusion, that others may see. Then will you be a "bringer of the light." Then will you be part of the Awakening, for it is possible to live in the physical body in conscious union with All That Is, in conscious awareness of ultimate truth; in conscious expression of Who You Really Are, and to serve as a model for all others who are living in forgetfulness.

Return to spirituality.

ESSENTIAL TRUTH:

Forget religion—it is not good for you. Understand that in order for organized religion to succeed, it has to make people believe they need it. In order for people to put faith in something else, they must first lose faith in themselves. So the first task of organized religion is to make you lose faith in yourself. The second task is to make you see that it has the answers you do not. And the third and most important task is to make you accept its answers without question.

If you question, you start to think! If you think, you start to go back to that Source Within. Religion can't have you do that, because you're liable to come up with an answer different from what it has contrived. So religion must make you doubt your Self, must make you doubt your own ability to think straight, must not have you living by your intuitive knowing

Religion has filled the hearts of men with fear of God; ordered men to bow down before God; burdened man with worries about God's wrath; told man to be ashamed of his body and most natural functions; taught that you must have an intermediary in order to reach God; commanded humans to adore God; and created disunity—which is the opposite of God. It has separated man from man, man from woman, and insists that God is above man—thus setting the stage for the greatest travesties ever foisted upon the human race.

Return to spirituality and believe in the goodness of God, and believe in the goodness of God's creation—namely, your holy Selves.

Absolute Power demands
absolutely nothing.

In my purest form, I am the Absolute. I am Absolutely everything, and therefore I need, want, and demand absolutely nothing. . . . Yet, no matter what you make of Me, I cannot forget, and will always return to, My Purest Form. . . .

You may come home whenever you wish. We can be together again whenever you want. The ecstasy of your union with Me is yours to know again. At the drop of a hat. At the feel of the wind on your face. At the sound of a cricket under diamond skies on a summer night. At the first sight of a rainbow and the first cry of a newborn babe. At the last ray of a spectacular sunset and the last breath in a spectacular life. I am with you always, even unto the end of time. Your union with Me is complete—it always was, always is, and always will be.

You and I are One—both now and even forevermore.

Go now, and make of your life a statement of this truth. Cause your days and nights to be reflections of the highest idea within you. Allow your moments of New to be filled with the spectacular ecstasy of God made manifest through you. Do it through the expression of your Love, eternal and unconditional, for all those whose lives you touch. Be a light unto the darkness, and curse it not.

Be a bringer of the light. You are that. So be it.

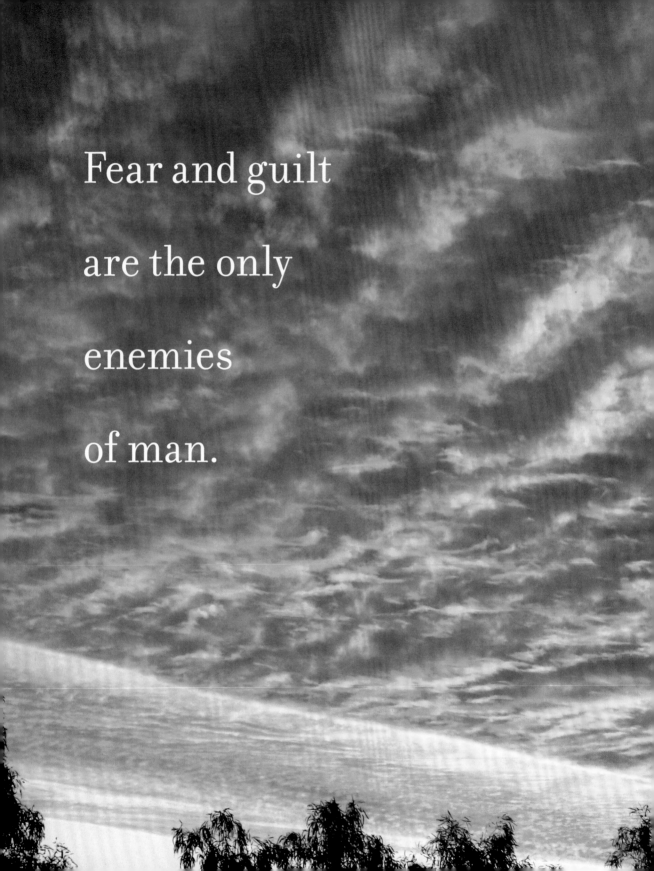

Fear and guilt

are the only

enemies

of man.

ESSENTIAL TRUTH:

Guilt is the feeling that keeps you stuck in who you are not. You will not grow through guilt, but only shrivel and die. Awareness is what you seek. But awareness is not guilt, and love is not fear. Fear and guilt are your enemies. Love and awareness are your true friends. Yet do not confuse the one with the other, for one will kill you, while the other gives you life.

Never, ever feel "guilty" about anything. What good is there in that? It only allows you to not love yourself—and that kills any chance that you could love another.

Fear nothing. Fear and caution are two different things. Be cautious—be conscious—but do not be fearful. For fear only paralyzes, while consciousness mobilizes. Be mobilized, not paralyzed.

If I could give you any gift, any special grace, that would allow you to find Me, it would be fearlessness. Blessed are the fearless, for they shall know God.

All states of mind
reproduce themselves.

ESSENTIAL TRUTH:

Most people have the process of creation (the Be-Do-Have paradigm) reversed. Most people believe if they "have" a thing, then they can finally "do" a thing, which will allow them to "be" a thing—like "happy." In the universe as it really is, "havingness" does not produce "being-ness," but the other way around.

The way to set this creative process into motion is to look at what it is you want to "have," ask yourself what you think you would "be" if you "had" that, then go right straight to being—for instance, "happy." In this way you reverse the way you've been using the Be-Do-Have paradigm—in actuality, set it right. You work with, rather than against, the creative power of the universe.

In life, you do not have to do anything. It is all a question of what you are being.

Deciding ahead of time what you choose to be produces that in your experience. Happiness (or knowing, or wisdom, or compassion, or whatever) is a state of mind. And like all states of mind, it reproduces itself in physical form. All states of mind reproduce themselves.

Whatever you choose for yourself,
give to another.

ESSENTIAL TRUTH:

However, your actions have to be sincere. Everything you do, do out of sincerity, or the benefit of the action is lost. Natural law requires the body, mind, and spirit to be united in thought, word, and action for the process of creation to work, and the mind seems very clear that God will bring good things through you to another.

If you choose to be happy, cause another to be happy. Praise and honor them.

If you choose to be prosperous, cause another to prosper.

If you choose more love in your life, cause another to have more love in theirs.

Do this sincerely—not because you seek personal gain, but because you really want the other person to have that—and all the things you give away will come to you.

The very act of your giving something away causes you to experience that you have it to give away—your mind comes to a new conclusion, a New Thought, about you. This becomes your experience and you start "being" that. You re-engaged the gears of the most powerful creation machine in the universe—your Divine Self.

Whatever you are being, you are creating. The circle is complete. When you give something to another with purity of heart—because you see that they want it, need it, and should have it—then you will discover that you have it to give. And that is a grand discovery.

I love you.

Do you know that?

All of it is the same thing.

ESSENTIAL TRUTH:

Life is all a matter of perspective. If you can see this truth, you will begin to understand the macro reality of God. And you will have unlocked a secret of the whole universe. Life is a series of minute, incredibly rapid movements. These movements do not affect at all the immobility of the Beingness of Everything That Is, such as the seemingly "unmoving" rock, whose subatomic particles of matter are racing around continually, even as the rock seems not to be moving.

The rock is moving and not moving at the same time. It is the movement which is creating the stillness, right before your eyes. There is no separateness. There cannot be, for All That Is is All There Is, and there is nothing else. From a distance it looks solid, not moving, but when you look very closely at what is actually happening, you see that everything that comprises the thing called "rock" is moving, at incredible speed through time and space in a particular pattern which creates the thing called "rock."

Which, then, is the illusion? The oneness, the stillness, of the rock, or the separateness and movement of its parts? Both observations are accurate. Both realities are "real." From the limited perspective with which you view All That Is, you see yourself as separate and apart, not as one unmovable being, but as many, many beings, constantly in motion. The rock will not be a rock forever. The same is true of you.

This is what the soul realizes at the moment of what you call "death." It is simply a change in perspective. You see more, so you understand more. You see the rock, and you see into the rock. Your perspective creates your thoughts, and your thoughts create everything—and if you can remember it before you leave the body, your whole life will change. Assume a different perspective and you will have a different thought about everything.

Life is not about power,
but about strength.

ESSENTIAL TRUTH:

It's not about separation, but unity. For it is in the unity that inner strength exists, and in the separation that it dissipates, leaving one feeling weak and powerless—and hence struggling for power. Power comes from inner strength. Inner strength does not come from raw power. In this most of the world has it backward.

This is true of the relationship between you and your God—just as it is remarkably true of the relationship between you and your fellow humans. Stop thinking of yourself as separate, and all the true power that comes from the inner strength of unity is yours—as a worldwide society, and as an individual part of that whole—to wield as you wish.

Heal the rift between you, end the illusion of separation, and you shall be delivered back to the source of your inner strength. That is where you will find true power—to do anything—be anything—have anything. For the power to create is derived from the inner strength that is produced through unity.

Power without inner strength is an illusion. Inner strength without unity is a lie, a lie that has not served the race. This lie is the genesis of all wars, and all the class struggles that lead to all wars; of all the animosity between races and genders, and all the power struggles that lead to animosity; of all personal trials and tribulations, and all the internal struggles that lead to tribulations. Still, you cling to the lie tenaciously.

Act as if you were separate from nothing and no one, and you will heal the world.

Understand that it is about power with, not power over. This is the greatest secret of all time.

The Eternal Moment contains all "possible possibilities."

Everything has already happened, in a million different ways.

All that's left is for you to make some perception choices.

It is all a question of perception.

When you change your perception,

you change your thought,

and your thought creates your reality.

Most of what you experience does not exist, yet you experience it nonetheless.

Essential Truth:

Hell does not exist. However, you create your own reality not only when you are with the body, but when you are away from it. In what you call the afterlife, you will instantly and automatically be surrounded by beings of high consciousness—and by high consciousness itself. Still, you may not know that you are being so lovingly enveloped; you may not immediately understand. In truth, you experience the consciousness in which you die.

Some of you have expectations without even knowing it. All your life you've had thoughts about what occurs after death, and when you "die" those thoughts are made manifest, and you suddenly realize (make real) what you've been thinking about. And it is your strongest thoughts, the ones you've held most fervently, that, as always in life, will prevail.

Nothing exists in Ultimate Reality save That Which Is. However, it is correct that you may create any sub-reality you choose—including the experience of hell as you describe it. You will experience after death exactly what you expect, and choose, to experience. But one thing you will come to know and understand very quickly is that you are at choice, always, about what you wish to experience. You will understand yourself to be creating your own reality. In the afterlife results are instantaneous, and you will not be able to miss the connection between your thoughts about a thing, and the experience those thoughts create.

God has never said that you could not experience hell; He said that hell does not exist.

All caused effect is
ultimately experienced
by the Self.

ESSENTIAL TRUTH:

There are no "rights" and "wrongs," no "do's" and "don'ts" in My world—and you do not burn in the everlasting fires of hell if you make a "bad" choice, because neither "bad" nor "hell" exists—unless, of course, you think it does!

Still, there are natural laws that have been built into the physical universe—and one of those is the law of cause and effect. One of the most important laws of cause and effect is this:

All caused effect is ultimately experienced by the Self.

This means that whatever you cause another to experience, you will one day experience: "What goes around, comes around." Others know this as the Jesus Injunction: Do unto others as you would have it done unto you. Jesus was teaching the law of cause and effect. It is what might be called the Prime Law.

You will return to the Oneness
many times.

ESSENTIAL TRUTH:

Grand realities and wondrous experiences await the joyous soul leaving the body. You may do one of three things in what you call the afterlife. Firstly, you may submit to the creations of your uncontrolled thoughts. Most will not do so for very long, and in the moment you don't like what you are experiencing, you will create a new and more pleasant reality by simply stopping your negative thoughts. You'll look back at this first stage and call it purgatory.

Secondly, you may create your experience consciously out of choice and you will experience going "straight to heaven," if you believe in heaven, or whatever you wish to experience if you do not. The second stage, when you can have anything you want with the speed of your thought, your wishes will get better and better—then you will believe in heaven!

Thirdly, you may experience the collective consciousness of All That Is. Should you take the third path, you will move very quickly into total acceptance, total peace, total joy, total awareness, and total love, for that is the consciousness of the collective. Then you will become one with the Oneness, and there will be nothing else except That Which You Are—which is All There Ever Was, until you decide that there should be something else. This third stage when you experience the bliss of the Oneness you'll call Nirvana. Many of you have had this experience very briefly in meditation and it is an indescribable ecstasy.

After you experience the Oneness for an infinite time—no time—you will cease to experience it, creating once again the idea of the thought of separation, or disunity. Then you will keep traveling on the Cosmic Wheel, forevermore. You will return to the Oneness an infinite number of times, for an infinite period each time—knowing that you have the tools to return to the Oneness at any point on the Cosmic Wheel. The process—this Cosmic Wheel—is a glorious and continual reaffirmation of the utter magnificence of God and all life.

Impermanence is the only truth.
Nothing is permanent.

All is changing.

In every instant.

In every moment.

Intuition
is the ear of the soul.

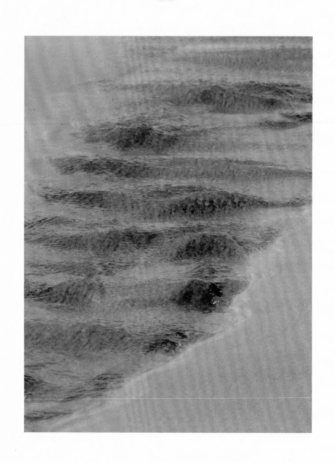

ESSENTIAL TRUTH:

You have six senses, not five. They are your senses of smell, taste, touch, sight, hearing, and . . . knowing. You all have what you call "psychic power." It is, truly, a sixth sense, and you all have a "sixth sense about things." It is simply the ability to step out of your limited experience into a broader view—to step back. To feel more than what the limited individual you have imagined yourself to be would feel; to know more than he or she would know. It is the ability to tap into the larger truth all around you; to sense a different energy.

To develop your psychic "muscle," you must exercise it. Use it every day, all the time. So when you get an intuitive "hit"—act on it. When you get a "hunch"—don't ignore it; have a dream or an inspiration—don't let it pass, paying it scant attention. Pay attention to every hunch you have, every feeling you feel, every intuitive "hit" you experience—pay attention. Then act on what you "know." Don't let your mind talk you out of it. Don't let your fear pull you away from it. The more you act on your intuition fearlessly, the more your intuition will serve you.

These energies are very light, very subtle. Like the slightest breeze on a summer night that you think you felt rustle your hair—but maybe didn't! To be psychic, you've got to be out of your mind, because intuition resides in the psyche—in the soul. The soul is the only instrument sensitive enough to "pick up" life's faintest vibrations, to sense these waves in the field, and to interpret them.

You are not what you were.

ESSENTIAL TRUTH:

You are not what you were, but are, and always will be, what you are now. You have based your sense of worthiness on the past, while I base your sense of worthiness on the future. That is where your life is, not in the past. The future. What you have done is unimportant compared to what you are about to do. How you have erred is insignificant compared to how you are about to create.

All of life is motion. Everything moves. Therefore, nothing is the same from one moment to the next. Remaining the same, or seeking to, moves against the laws of life. This is foolish, because in this struggle, life will always win. Change your ideas of right and wrong; your notions of this and that; your structures, constructions, models, and theories. Allow your deepest truths to be altered. Because your new idea of Who You Are is where the growth is. Your new idea of the Who, What, Where, When, How, and Why of it is where the mystery gets solved, the plot unravels, the story ends.

Your new idea about all of it is where the excitement is, the creation is, where God-in-you is made manifest and becomes fully realized.

No matter how "good" you think things have been, they can be better. No matter how wonderful you think your theologies, your ideologies, your cosmologies, they can be full of even more wonder. Be *open*. Don't close off the possibility of new truth because you have been comfortable with an old one. Life begins at the end of your comfort zone.

For you are all, all, in the process of becoming.

You are all, all, moving through the experience of evolution.

Love
is the best
"medium" of
communication.

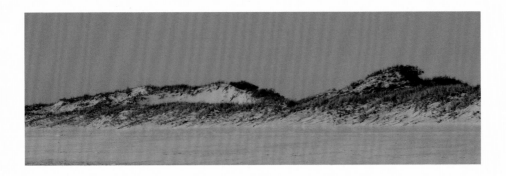

ESSENTIAL TRUTH:

The slightest thought having to do with a being existing on what you call the "other side" brings that being's consciousness flying to you. You cannot have a thought or an idea about a person who is what you call "deceased" without that person's Essence becoming completely aware of it. It is not necessary to use a medium to produce such communication. Love is the best "medium" of communication.

Loved ones are never far from you, never more than a thought away, and will always be there if you need them, ready with counsel or comfort or advice. Souls who loved you in this life are drawn to you, pulled to you, fly to you, the moment they sense the slightest trouble or disturbance in your auric field. If part of what they want to do is to come back to you—to see how you are, to bring you an awareness that they're all right, whatever—trust that they'll do that. One of their first opportunities, as they learn about the possibilities of their new existence, is to provide aid and comfort to those they love. And you will feel their comforting presence if you are really open to them. Watch for the "sign" and catch it. Don't dismiss it as just your imagination, "wishful thinking," or coincidence.

You have to see, feel, touch before you will believe. Yet that which you wish to know cannot be seen, felt, or touched. It is of another realm.

Reincarnation
is a fact.

Essential Truth:

Reincarnation—returning to another physical body—is a fact. Without reincarnation, the soul would have to accomplish everything it seeks to accomplish within one lifetime, which is one billion times shorter than the blink of an eye on the cosmic clock.

The process we are discussing here is evolution. Self-creation and evolution. And evolution proceeds one way—upward. The soul's greatest desire is to experience higher and higher aspects of itself. And so it seeks to move upward, not downward, on the evolutionary scale, until it experiences total Oneness with the All. If the soul returns to human form, it is always in an effort to further experience and thus further evolve. One could come back for many hundreds of lifetimes and continue to evolve upward.

After what you call your death, some souls feel that there is a lot more they would like to know, and so they find themselves going to a "school," where other souls—what you call "old souls"—teach them. And what do they teach them?

That they have nothing to learn.

That they never had anything to learn. That all they ever had to do was remember. Remember Who and What They Really Are. They are "taught" that the experience of Who They Are is gained in the acting out of it, in being it. Reincarnation—it's real, it's purposeful, and it's perfect.

THE GAME

The game does go on. Because one or two of you end
the cycle of illusion, that does not end the game—not for you,
and not for the other players.

The game is not ended until All-in-All becomes One again.
Even then it is not ended. For in the moment of divine reunion,
All with All, will the bliss be so magnificent, so intense, that I-We-You
will literally burst wide open with gladness, exploding with joy—
and the cycle will begin all over again.

It will never end, My child. The game will never end.
For the game is life itself,
and life is Who We Are.

Nothing is painful
which you understand
is not real.

258

ESSENTIAL TRUTH:

When you understand that life is eternal, you understand that death is your illusion, keeping you very concerned with, and therefore helping you believe that you are your body. Yet you are not your body, and so the destruction of your body is of no concern to you.

Nothing is painful the moment you understand that nothing is real. This is as true of death as it is of life. Death is never an end, but always a beginning. A death is a door opening, not a door closing. Life cannot give itself to you if you do not understand death. You must do more than understand it, you must love it, even as you love life.

Your time with each person would be glorified if you thought it was your last time with that person. Your experience of each moment would be enhanced beyond measure if you thought it was the last moment. Your refusal to contemplate your own death leads to your refusal to contemplate your own life. You miss the moment, and all it holds for you.

When you look deeply at something, you see right through it. Then the illusion ceases to exist—you see a thing for what it really is. Even the illusion you can then enjoy. For you will know it is an illusion, and that is half the enjoyment! It is the fact that you think it is real that causes you all the pain. It is like a movie, a drama, played out on the stage of your mind. You are creating the situation and the characters. You are writing the lines.

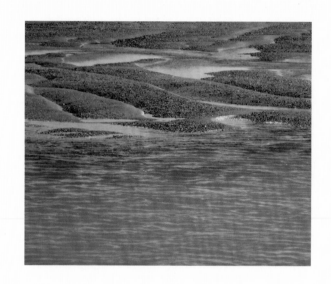

The state of true wakefulness.

ESSENTIAL TRUTH:

Use your life as a meditation, and all the events in it. Walk in wakefulness, not as one asleep. Move with mindfulness, not mindlessly. In meditation you place yourself in a state of readiness to experience total awareness (of knowing Who You Really Are) while your body is in a wakened state. This state of readiness is called true wakefulness.

Meditation is simply a "tool," but you do not have to be sitting in meditation to experience this—it's not the only kind of meditation there is. There is also stopping meditation, walking meditation, doing meditation, sexual meditation.

When you stop in this state, simply stop in your tracks, stop going where you are going, stop doing what you are doing, just stop for a moment and just "be" right where you are. Look around slowly and notice things you did not notice while you were passing them by. The deep smell of the earth, how good it feels to see a child at play. You don't have to leave your body to experience this. This is the state of true wakefulness.

When you walk in this state, breathe in every flower's scent, fly with every bird, feel every crunch beneath your feet—find beauty and wisdom, out of all the stuff of life. You don't have to leave your body to experience this. This is the state of true wakefulness.

When you "do" in this state, you turn whatever you are doing into a meditation, and thus into a gift, from you to your soul, and from your soul to the All. While washing dishes, enjoy the warm water caressing your hands. While working on your computer, see the words appear on the screen and exhilarate over the power of the mind and body. While preparing dinner, feel the love of the universe which brought you this nourishment, and pour love into the making of the meal, no matter how simple. You don't have to leave your body to experience this. This is the state of true wakefulness.

When you experience sexual energy exchange in this state, you know the highest truth of Who You Are.

A smile can take you there. Just stop everything for one moment and smile. At nothing. Just because it feels good. Smile a lot. It will cure whatever ails you.

Breathe—long and deep—slowly and gently. Breathe in the soft, sweet nothingness of life, so full of energy, so full of love. It is God's love you are breathing, and you can feel it. Breathe very, very deeply, and the love will make you cry—for joy. For you have met your God, and your God has introduced you to your soul.

All of life is a meditation, in which you are contemplating the Divine. This is called true wakefulness, or mindfulness, and, experienced in this way, everything in life is blessed.

What would happen
if everyone did it?

ESSENTIAL TRUTH:

If you want a yardstick with which to judge whether a thing is good for the human race or not, ask yourself a simple question:

What would happen if everyone did it?

This is a very easy measure, and a very accurate one.

If everyone did a thing, and the result would be of ultimate benefit to the human race, then that is "evolved." If everyone did it and it would bring disaster to the human race, then that is not a very "elevated" thing to recommend.

Glorify what you are today,
yet do not condemn what
you were yesterday,
nor preclude what you
could become tomorrow.

There is only One of us.
There are Many of us.

ESSENTIAL TRUTH:

We are all the same energy, coalesced, compressed in different ways to create different forms and different matter. Your scientists are already discovering that the building blocks of all of life are the same. They brought back rocks from the moon and found the same stuff they find in trees. They take apart a tree and find the same stuff they find in you. We are all the same stuff.

There is only One Being, and hence only One Soul. And there are many souls in the One Being. While there is no actual separation between souls, it is true that the stuff of which the One Soul is made manifests in physical reality at different speeds, producing different degrees of density. All of life is a vibration—pure energy. That energy is vibrating constantly, always—moving in waves. The waves vibrate at different speeds, producing different degrees of density, or light. This, in turn, produces what you would call different "effects" in the physical world—actually, different physical objects. Yet while the objects are different and discreet, the energy which produces them is exactly the same.

Like the air in your house, the energy of life takes on different characteristics as it surrounds different physical objects. Indeed, that energy coalesces in a particular way to form those objects. As particles of energy join together to form physical matter, they become very concentrated—mashed up—pushed together. They begin to "look like," even "feel like," distinct units. That is, they begin to seem "separate," "different" from all the other energy. Yet this is all the same energy, behaving differently. It is this very act of behaving differently which makes it possible for That Which Is All to manifest as That Which Is Many.

The "elements of energy" which coalesced into discrete units that held in physical beings are what you have chosen to call "souls." The parts of Me that have become the lot of You are what We are talking about here. The Great Mystery, the eternal truth.

There is only One of Us, and so, it is THAT WHICH YOU ARE.

No matter
is inconsequential.

ESSENTIAL TRUTH:

Every act is an act of self-definition. Everything you think, say, and do declares, "This is Who I Am." You are all in the process of defining yourselves. If you are pleased with how you have created yourself, if it serves you, you will continue doing so in that way. If you are not, you will stop. This is called evolution.

If it serves you to go to war and kill other beings, you will do so. If it serves you to terminate a pregnancy, you will do so. The only thing that changes as you evolve is your idea of what serves you. And that is based on what you think you are trying to do. If you are trying to get to Seattle, it will not serve you to head toward San Jose.

The question of what you are trying to do, then, becomes a question of prime importance. Not just in your life in general, but in every moment of your life specifically. Because it is in the moments of life that a life itself is created.

When you are preparing to have your abortion, therefore, or smoke that cigarette, or fry and eat that animal, and when you are preparing to cut that man off in traffic—whether the matter is large or small, major or minor—there is only one question to consider: Is this Who I Really Am? Is this who I now choose to be?

No matter is inconsequential. There is a consequence to everything. The consequence is who and what you are. That is your answer to every question about behavior you've ever had.

You are defining God.

Essential Truth:

All your life you have been told that God created you. I come now to tell you: You are creating God. In every moment God expresses Himself in, as, and through you. You are always at choice as to how God will be created now, and She will never take that choice from you, nor will She punish you for making the "wrong" choice. Yet you are not without guidance in these matters, nor will you ever be. Built into you is an internal guidance system that shows you the way home. This is the voice that speaks to you always of your highest choice, that places before you your grandest vision. All you need to do is heed that voice, and not abandon the vision.

Holy scriptures have been written, and holy lives have been lived, that you might know of this eternal truth: You and I are One.

Who you are, I am. You are defining God.

I have sent you—a blessed part of Me—into physical form that I might know Myself experientially as all that I know Myself to be conceptually. Life exists as a tool for God to turn concept into experience. It exists for you to do the same. For you are God, doing this.

I choose to re-create Myself anew in every single moment. I choose to experience the grandest version of the greatest vision ever I had about Who I Am. I have created you, so that you might re-create Me. This is Our very reason for being.

The first guiding principle
of advanced civilizations
is *unity*.

Essential Truth:

The first guiding principle of advanced civilization is unity—acknowledgment of the Oneness, and the sacredness of all life. Highly evolved beings (HEBs) live in unity, and with a deep sense of interrelatedness. Their behaviors are created by their Sponsoring Thoughts—what you might call the basic guiding principles of their society.

Their First Guiding Principle is: We Are All One. Every decision, every choice, all of what you would call "morals" and "ethics," is based upon this principle.

The Second Guiding Principle is: Everything in the One Interrelates. Under this principle, no one member of a species could, or would, keep something from another simply because "he had it first," or it's his "possession," or it's in "short supply." The mutual dependency of all living things in the species system is recognized and honored. The relative needs of every species of living organism within the system are always kept in balance—because they are always kept in mind.

A HEB experiences "personal ownership" in the sense of holding personal responsibility for every good thing in his care. A HEB is a steward, not an owner. That is, HEBs hold, embrace, love, and care for things, but do not own them.

Humans possess, HEBs caress.

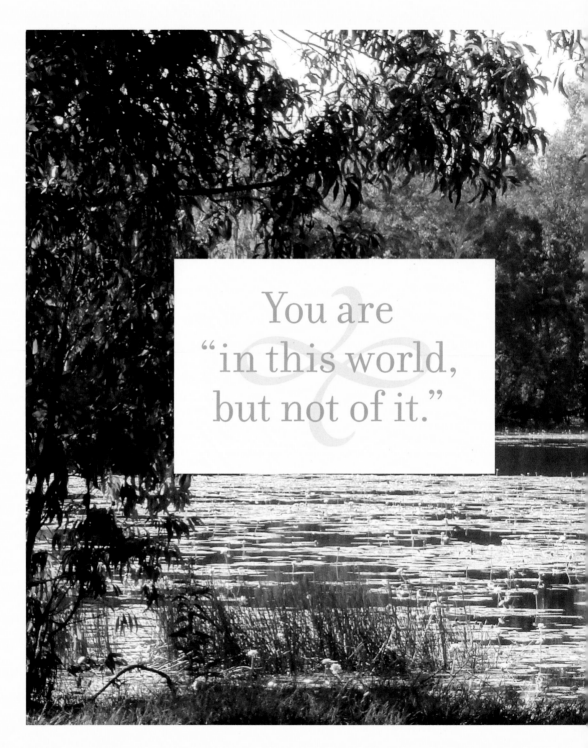

You are
"in this world,
but not of it."

274

Highly evolved

civilizations and highly

evolved beings . . . *share.*

ESSENTIAL TRUTH:

They share everything. With everyone. Not a being goes without. All the natural resources of their world, of their environment, are divided equally and distributed to everyone.

A nation or a group or a culture isn't thought to "own" a natural resource simply because it happens to occupy the physical location where that resource is found. The planet (or planets) which a group of species calls "home" is understood to belong to everyone—to all the species in that system. Indeed, the planet or group of planets itself is understood to be a "system." It is viewed as a whole system, not as a bunch of little parts or elements, any one of which can be eliminated, decimated, or eradicated without damage to the system itself.

It's not just the ecology—which is the relationship of the planet's natural resources to the planet's inhabitants. It's also the relationship of the inhabitants to themselves, to each other, and to the environment. It's the interrelationship of all the species of life.

It is understood that the species system supports all life, and every being, at the optimum level. Doing nothing that would harm the species system is therefore a statement that each individual being is important. Not only the individual beings with status or influence or money. Not only the individual beings with power or size or the presumption of greater self-awareness. All beings, and all species, in the system.

Highly evolved beings . . .

live a lot longer.

ESSENTIAL TRUTH:

How much longer? Many times longer.

In some HEB societies, beings live forever—or as long as they choose to remain in corporeal form. Of course, they are never not alive, any more than you are. So in HEB societies, individual beings are usually around to experience the long-term consequences of their actions.

How is this possible? Well, first, because they don't pollute their air, their water, and their land. They do not put chemicals into the ground, which are then taken up by plants and animals and brought into the body upon consumption of those plants and animals. A HEB, in fact, would never consume an animal, much less fill the ground and the plants which the animal eats with chemicals, then fill the animal itself with chemicals and then consume it. A HEB would correctly assess such a practice to be suicidal. So HEBs do not pollute their environment, their atmosphere, or their own corporeal bodies, as humans do.

HEBs also exhibit different psychological behaviors that equally prolong life. A HEB never worries—and wouldn't even understand the human concept of "worry" or "stress." Neither would a HEB "hate," or feel "rage," or "jealousy," or "panic." Therefore, the HEB does not produce biochemical reactions within her own body that eat away at it and destroy it.

A HEB understands that all things are perfect, that there is a process in the universe that is working itself out, and that all they have to do is not interfere with it. So a HEB never worries, because a HEB understands the process. A HEB finds life in the body enjoyable and can't imagine doing anything that she knows ahead of time would limit or terminate that, or make it painful. Your bodies are magnificent creations, made to "last" infinitely longer than you allow them to.

In highly evolved societies,
there is *no shame*,
nor any such thing as guilt.

Essential Truth:

In highly evolved cultures, beings would never be asked to do something they've demonstrated an inability to do. Their own demonstrated inability would eliminate their desire to "want" to. This is a natural outcome of their understanding that their inability to do a particular thing could potentially damage another. This they would never do, for to damage the Other is to damage the Self, and they know this.

A human defines Self very narrowly. You speak of your Self, your family, your community. A HEB defines Self quite differently. She speaks of the Self, the family, the community. And so, in a highly evolved culture, a being would never, for instance, insist on raising offspring if that being consistently demonstrated to itself its own inability to do so.

Also, a HEB does not feel guilt or shame, because guilt and shame are concepts which are imposed on a being from outside of itself. They can then be internalized, no question about that, but they are initially imposed from the outside. Always. No divine being (and all beings are divine) ever knows Itself or anything it is doing to be "shameful" or "guilty" until someone outside of Itself labels it that way.

The degree to which a culture is evolved is demonstrated by the degree to which it labels a being or an action "shameful" or "guilty."

Highly evolved cultures . . .
do not compete.

ESSENTIAL TRUTH:

They realize that when one loses, everyone loses.

They therefore do not create sports and games which teach children (and perpetuate in adults) the extraordinary thought that someone "winning" while another is "losing" is entertainment.

Survival of the Fittest underlies everything your society has created—its economics, its politics, its religions, its education, and its social structures. Yet to a highly evolved being the principle itself is an oxymoron. It is self-contradictory. Since the First Guiding Principle of a HEB is We Are All One, the "One" is not "fit" until the "All" is "fit." Survival of the "fittest" is, therefore, impossible—or the only thing that is possible (therefore a contradiction)—since the "fittest" is not "fit" until it is.

On your planet you have rejected out-of-hand any system which does not allow for the advancement of one being at the expense of another.

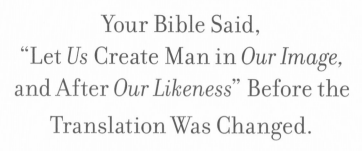

Your Bible Said, "Let *Us* Create Man in *Our Image*, and After *Our Likeness*" Before the Translation Was Changed.

Life is the process through which God creates Itself, and then experiences the creation. This process of creation is ongoing and eternal. It is happening all the "time." Relativity and physicality are the tools with which God works. Pure energy (what you call spirit) is What God Is. This Essence is truly the Holy Spirit.

By a process through which energy becomes matter, spirit is embodied in physicality. This is done by the energy literally slowing itself down—changing its oscillation, or what you would call vibration.

That Which Is All does this in parts. That is, parts of the whole do this. These individuations of spirit are what you have chosen to call souls. In truth, there is only One Soul, reshaping and re-forming Itself. This might be called the Reformation. You are all Gods in Formation. (God's *information!*) That is your contribution, and it is sufficient unto itself. To put this simply, by taking physical form *you have already done enough*. I want, I need, nothing more.

In highly evolved cultures there is no concept of "*yours*" and "*mine*."

ESSENTIAL TRUTH:

A distinguishing feature of highly evolved cultures is that within them there is no word or sound for, nor any way to communicate the meaning of, the concept of "yours" and "mine." Personal possessives do not exist in their language, and if one were to speak in earthly tongues, one could only use articles to describe things. Employing that convention, "my car" becomes "the car I am now with." "My partner" or "my children" become "the partner" or "the children I am now with." The term "now with," or "in the presence of," is as close as your languages can come to describing what you would call "ownership" or "possession."

That which you are "in the presence of" becomes the Gift. These are the true "presents" of life. Thus, in the language of highly evolved cultures, one would not even speak in terms of "my life," but could only communicate "the life I am in the presence of." This is something akin to your speaking of being "in the presence of God."

When you are in the presence of God (which you are, anytime you are in the presence of each other), you would never think of keeping from God that which is God's—meaning, any part of That Which Is. You would naturally share, and share equally, that which is God's with any part of that which is God. This is the spiritual understanding which undergirds the entire social, political, economic, and religious structures of all highly evolved cultures. This is the cosmology of all of life.

Until your
*community of
beings* knows
about *being
in community*,
you will never
experience Holy
Communion,
and cannot know
Who I Am.

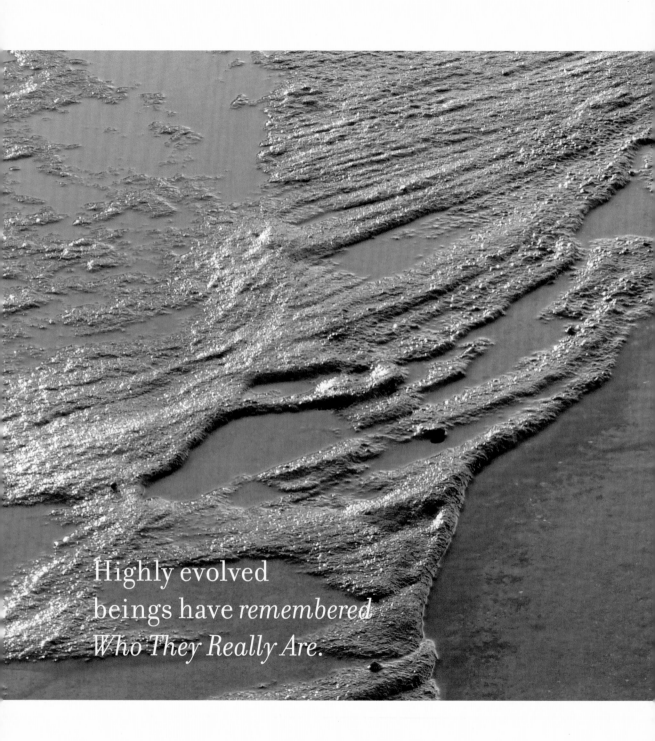

Highly evolved
beings have *remembered*
Who They Really Are.

ESSENTIAL TRUTH:

Therefore . . .

- As for what you call "work," such a concept does not exist in most HEB cultures. Tasks are performed and activities undertaken, based purely on what a being loves to do and sees as the highest expression of Self. The concept of "menial labor" does not exist. HEBs who do the daily tasks that "must" be done for a society to exist and to function are the most highly rewarded, highly decorated in the service of All, and what they do is considered the highest form of self-fulfillment.

- Technology has advanced in HEB societies. In addition to what has been provided by new physical technologies, understandings of the mind and of the very nature of physicality itself have also advanced. As a result of the combination of these two types of evolutionary advances, it has become possible for HEBs to disassemble and reassemble their bodies at will, allowing most beings in most highly evolved cultures to "be" wherever they choose—whenever they choose.

- The concept of "success" as you have defined it is foreign to a HEB, precisely because its opposite—failure—does not exist. Achieving is defined as "doing what brings value," not "doing what brings fame and fortune, whether it is of value of not." HEBs value that which produces benefit to All. They always see "what's so," and do "what works"—given where they choose for their society to go.

- There are no "have nots" in a HEB society. There is no such thing as "the destitute" and "the poor." They avoid that by applying two basic principles: We are all One and There's Enough. HEBs have an awareness of sufficiency, and a consciousness that creates it. If you would change these two elements of your consciousness, everything would shift.

Evolution is the process.

Essential Truth:

Most people think that "evolution" is a process which is simply "going on"—not a process which they are *directing*, according to certain *principles*. All races and species are evolving, and evolution (the purpose of observing what serves you, and making behavioral adaptions), seems to be moving toward unity, and away from separation. Unity is the Ultimate Truth, and "evolution" is just another word for "movement toward truth."

So the *process* is called "evolution." The "principle" which *guides* the process is what directs the course of your evolution. Evolution is "survival of the fittest." That is the *process*. Yet do not confuse "process" and "principle." If "evolution" and "survival of the fittest" are synonymous, and if you are claiming "survival of the fittest" as a Guiding Principle, then you are saying, "A Guiding Principle of Evolution is *evolution*."

That is the statement of a race which does not know that it can *control the course of its own evolution*. That is the statement of a species which thinks itself to be relegated to the status of observer of its own evolution. And so the species is announcing, "We evolve by the principle of . . . well, *evolution*." But they never say what that principle *is*, because they have confused the process and the principle.

The species, on the other hand, which has become clear that evolution is a process— but a process *over which the species has control*—has not confused "process" with "principle," but consciously *chooses* a principle which it *uses to guide and direct its process*. This is called *conscious evolution* and your species has just arrived there.

Highly evolved beings do not use "evolution" as their First Guiding Principle of Evolution, but, rather, they have *created* a principle, based on pure observation. They have simply observed that they are all One, and they have devised political, social, economic, and spiritual mechanisms which *undergird*, rather than undermine, that First Principle.

Yours is a race awakening.

ESSENTIAL TRUTH:

I have described your culture as primitive. "Primitive" is merely descriptive. It simply says what is true: a certain thing is in the very early stages of development—nothing more than that. It's merely an observation of What Is.

I want you to know that I love you. I have no judgments about you. I look at you and see only beauty and wonder. I hear your melody and I feel only excitement.

I am aroused to new possibilities, to new experiences yet to come. In you I am awakened to new adventures, and to the excitement of movement to new levels of magnificence. You think you are at the pinnacle of human development and I tell you, *you are just beginning.* You have only just begun to experience your splendor! Your grandest ideas are as yet unexpressed, and your grandest vision unlived.

I see a new force for change growing in intensity on your planet. Entire thought systems are being abandoned. Economic policies are being revised. Spiritual truths are being reexamined. *Yours in a race awakening.*

Embody the consciousness of "We Are All One," and "There's Enough." Change your Self, change the world. You have a chance now to re-create the best experiences of your ancient civilizations, while avoiding the worst. You don't have to let personal egos and advanced technology destroy your society this time. You can do it differently. You—you—*can make a difference.*

The Soul

The soul is *everywhere* in, through, and around you. It is that which *contains* you.

The soul is *larger than the body*. It is not carried within the body, but carries the body within *it*.

The soul is that which holds you together—just as *the Soul of God is that which contains the universe, and holds it together.*

The "Soul of God" holds in the universe, the "soul of man" holds in each individual human body.

Highly evolved beings . . . *deny nothing.*

Essential Truth:

In highly evolved cultures adults understand that children do what they see others doing. The Triangular Code—*Awareness, Honesty, Responsibility*—is not something which is "pounded into" the young HEB, but something which is acquired—almost by osmosis—through the behaviors *modeled* for the "child" by "adults."

It would never occur to HEBs to place their offspring for many hours in front of a device that shows pictures of behaviors they'd like their offspring to avoid. Such a decision would be incomprehensible. Equally incomprehensible, if a HEB *did* do this, would be to deny that the pictures had anything to do with their offsprings' suddenly aberrant behaviors. The difference between HEB society and human society breaks down to one really very simple element, which we shall call truthful observation.

In HEB societies, beings acknowledge everything they see. In human societies, many deny what they see. They see television ruining their children, and they ignore it. They see violence and "losing" used as "entertainment," and deny the contradiction. They observe that tobacco harms the body, and pretend it does not. They see a father who is drunken and abusive, and the whole family denies it, letting no one say a word about it. They observe that their religions have failed utterly to change mass behaviors, and deny this. They see that their governments do more to oppress than to assist, and they ignore it. They see a health-care system that is really a disease-care system. They see that eating the flesh of animals that have been slaughtered after having been force-fed chemical-laden foods is not doing their health any good, yet they deny what they see.

Highly evolved beings—which some of you are becoming—deny *nothing*. They observe "what's so." They see clearly "what works." Using these simple tools, life becomes simple. "The Process" is honored.

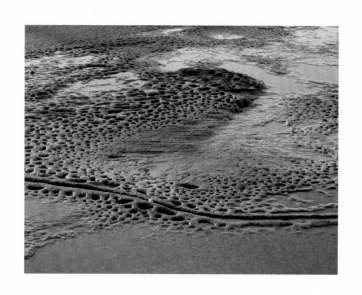

Jesus was a highly

evolved being.

ESSENTIAL TRUTH:

If the beings from highly advanced cultures were to share with you some technologies, these would be given in a way, and at a rate, which would allow you to recognize your *own* powers and potentials, not those of another. Similarly, if HEBs were to share with you some teachings, these, too, would be shared in a way, and at a rate, that would allow you to see greater truths, and your *own* powers and potentials, and *not make gods of your teachers.*

You are all evolving beings. Some of you are highly evolved. That is, you *re-member more.* You know Who You Really Are. Jesus knew it, and declared it. The spirit of that human you call Jesus was not of this Earth. That spirit simply filled a human body, allowed itself to learn as a child, become a man and self-realized. He was not the only one to have done this. *All spirits* are "not of this Earth." *All souls* come from another realm, then enter the body. Yet not all souls self-realize in a particular "lifetime." Jesus did. He was a highly evolved being and he came to you for a purpose, on a mission.

His mission was—is—to save you from not knowing and never experiencing Who You Really Are. His intention was to demonstrate that by showing you what you can become. Indeed, what you are—if you will only accept it. Jesus sought to lead by example, in the sense that you would all *follow his example* and *become one with God.* He said, "I and the Father are One, and ye are my brethren." He couldn't have put it more plainly.

*Caring creates
communication.*

ESSENTIAL TRUTH:

The differences between human cultures and highly evolved cultures is that highly evolved beings:

Observe fully and *communicate truthfully*.

They see "what works" and say "what's so." The discussion is always around what works for a HEB society—what is functional and produces benefit for all—not around what humans would call "right" and "wrong." Honestly expressing one's feelings, for example, is often deemed by human society as "wrong." Such a conclusion could never be arrived at by a HEB, since precise awareness of feelings facilitates *life* in any community. It would be impossible in any event, because a HEB receives "vibes"—actual *vibrations*—from other beings, which make their feelings plain enough.

Actual utterances—what you would call "words"—are rarely, if ever, used. This "telepathic communication" occurs between all highly evolved sentient beings. Indeed, it could be said that the degree to which a species—or a relationship between members of the same species—has evolved is demonstrated by the degree to which beings require the use of "words" to convey feelings, desires, or information.

But many of you are returning to a cleaner form of communication, more accurate and more elegant. This is especially true between loved ones—emphasizing a major truth: *caring creates communication*. Where there is deep love, words are virtually unnecessary. The reverse of this axiom is also true: the more words you *have* to use with each other, the less time you must be taking to care for each other, because caring creates communication. Ultimately, all real communication is about truth. And ultimately, the only real truth is love. That is why, when love is present, so is communication.

You cannot have advanced technologies in any beneficial way without advanced thinking.

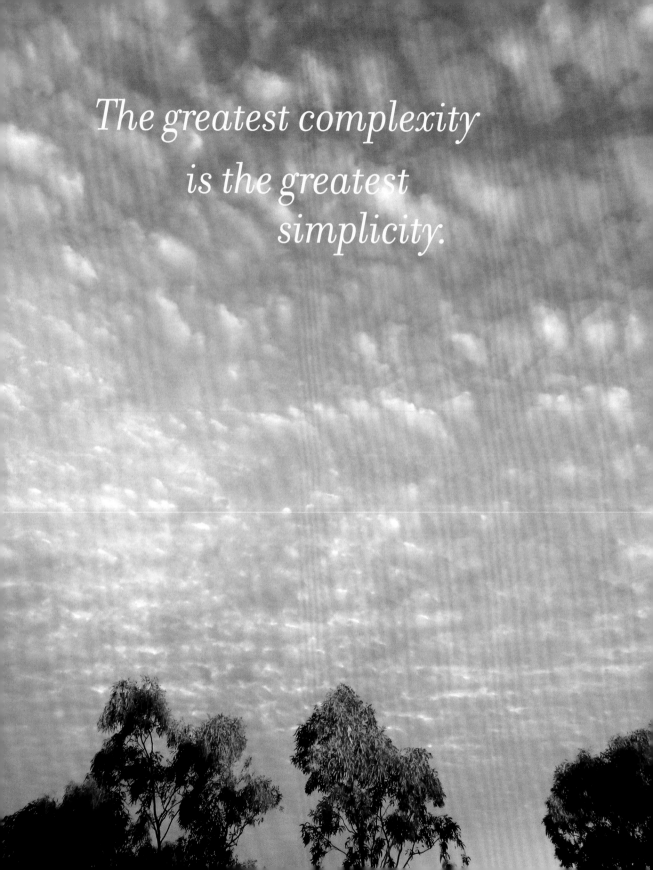

The greatest complexity is the greatest simplicity.

ESSENTIAL TRUTH:

It is the mark of a primitive culture to imagine that simplicity is barbarian, and complexity is highly advanced. Those who are highly advanced see it as being just the other way around. Yet here is the greatest Divine Dichotomy: *The greatest complexity is the greatest simplicity.*

The more "complex" a system is, the more simple is its design. Indeed, it is utterly elegant in its Simplicity.

The Master understands this. That is why a highly evolved being lives in utter simplicity. It is why all highly evolved systems are also utterly simple. Highly evolved systems of governance, highly evolved systems of education, highly evolved systems of economics or religion—all are utterly, elegantly simple. Highly evolved systems of governance, for instance, involve virtually *no governance at all,* save self-governance. As if there were only *one* being participating, as if there were only *one* being affected—which is all there is. Highly evolved cultures understand this because they have simply observed that they are all One.

There is something I do not know, the knowing of which could change everything.

God is a Process.

ESSENTIAL TRUTH:

Life is the Process by which everything is being created. God is the energy—the pure, raw energy—which you call life. By this awareness we come to a new truth. *God is a Process.* God is also the Process by which All is created, and experiences itself.

God is not a person, place, or thing. God is exactly what you have always thought—but not understood. You have always thought that God is the *Supreme* Being. And you have been right about that. I am exactly that. A BEING. Notice that "being" is not a thing, it is a process. I am the Supreme Being. That is, the Supreme, comma, *being*. I am not the *result* of a process; I am the Process Itself. I am the Creator, and I am the *Process by which I am created.*

Everything you see in the heavens and the earth is Me, being *created*. The Process of Creation is never over. It is never complete. I am never "done." This is another way of saying everything is forever changing. Nothing stands still. Nothing—*nothing*—is without motion. Everything is energy, in motion. You have called this "e-motion!" *You are God's highest emotion!*

When you look at a thing, you are not looking at a static "something" that is "standing there" in time and space. You are *witnessing an event*, because everything is moving, changing, evolving. *Everything*. God is an event. You have called that event *life*. Life is a Process. That Process is observable, knowable, predictable. The more you observe, the more you know, and the more you can predict. The One Unchanging Truth is that God is always changing. The one thing that never changes is that everything is always changing. Life is change. God is *life*, therefore, God is change.

"Before the cock crows,
you will deny Me three times."

ESSENTIAL TRUTH:

You've spent a lifetime denying Who and What You Really Are. You see goodness and compassion within you, but you deny it. You see wisdom within you, but you deny it. You see infinite possibility within you, but you deny it. And you see and experience God within you, yet you deny it. You deny that I am within you—that I *am* you—and in this you deny Me My rightful and obvious place.

I tell you this: "Before the cock crows, you will deny Me three times."

By your very thoughts will you deny Me. Every thought of your Self as smaller than you really are is a denial of Me.

By your very words will you deny Me. Every word about your Self that puts you down is a denial of Me.

By your very actions will you deny Me. Every action flowing through your Self that plays out a role of "not-good-enough," or lack, or insufficiency of any kind, is a denial indeed. Not just in thought, not just in word, but in deed.

You *know in your heart* that I am with you, in you; that We are One. Yet you deny Me. You say I exist, all right, but away from you. Way out there somewhere. And the farther away you imagine Me to be, the farther away you step from your own truth.

Do not allow your life to represent *anything* but the grandest version of the greatest vision you ever had about Who You Are. Now, what is the greatest vision you've ever had for your Self?

The Secret of All Life:

You not only *interpret* energy, you create it. Imagination is a function of your mind, which is one-third of your three-part being. In your mind you image something, and it begins to take form. The longer you imagine it (and the more *of you* who image it), the more physical that form becomes, until the increasing energy you have given it literally *bursts into light,* flashing an image of itself into what you call your reality.

You then "see" the image, and once again *decide what it is.* Thus, the cycle continues. This is what I have called the Process.

This is what YOU ARE. You ARE this Process.

This is what God IS, God IS this Process.

This is what I have meant when I have said, you are *both the Creator and the Created.*

I have now brought it all together for you . . . I have explained to you the mechanics of the universe, the secret of all life.

Observe.
Observe.
OBSERVE.

ESSENTIAL TRUTH:

Even though all beings have already lived through all contrasting experiences, some *do not know it*. They have forgotten, and have not yet moved into full remembering.

Highly evolved beings do not require "evil" or "negativity" in their own society. It is not necessary to have "negativity" right in front of them, in their own world, for them to know how "positive" their civilization is. They are "positively aware" of Who They Are without having to create negativity to prove it. HEBs merely notice who they are *not* by observing it *elsewhere in the contextual field*. Your own planet is one to which HEBs look if they seek a contrasting field—they are reminded of how it was when they experienced what you are now experiencing, and thus form an ongoing frame of reference.

You *do* have to live within a contextual field within which That Which You Are Not exists, in order for you to experience That Which You Are. This is the Universal Law, and you cannot avoid it. Yet you *are* living in such a field, right now. You do not have to create one. The contextual field in which you are living is called *the universe. You do not have to create a smaller contextual field in your own backyard.*

This means that you can change life on your planet right now, and eliminate all that you are not, without endangering in any way your ability to know and experience That Which You Are. You do not have to create the opposite of Who You Are and What You Choose in order to experience it. You merely need to observe that it has already been created—elsewhere. You need only remember that it exists. And to remember that it exists, to remember that you have experienced it all before—everything that is—in physical form . . . all you have to do is look up. LOOK UP to the stars, to the heavens. OBSERVE THE CONTEXTUAL FIELD.

All you need to do to become highly evolved beings is to increase *your observational skills.* See "what's so," and then do "what works."

No one can create your experience of anything.

Essential Truth:

Like the things life keeps bringing you!

Know and understand that you are bringing it to your Self.

SEE THE PERFECTION.

See it in *everything*, not just in things that you call perfect.

No one can create your experience of anything.

Other beings can, and *do*, co-create the exterior circumstances and events of the life you live in common, but *the one thing that no one else can do is cause you to have an experience* of ANYTHING you do not choose to experience.

In this, you are a Supreme being. And no one—NO ONE—can tell you "how to be."

The world can present you with circumstances, but only you decide what those circumstances mean.

Remember the truth I gave you long ago.

Nothing matters—*life resolves itself in the process of life itself.*

If you will just *let go,* you will have gotten yourself out of the "way." The "way" is the Process—which is called *life itself.* All wisdom asks you to do is trust the Process. That is, *trust God.* Or, if you wish, *trust yourself,* for Thou Art God.

Enjoy the Experience of Becoming.

The game would be over if you remembered everything. You came here for a particular reason, and your Divine Purpose would be thwarted if you understood how everything is put together. Some things will always remain a mystery at this level of consciousness and it is right that they should. So do not try to solve all the mysteries. They will unfold itself in due course.

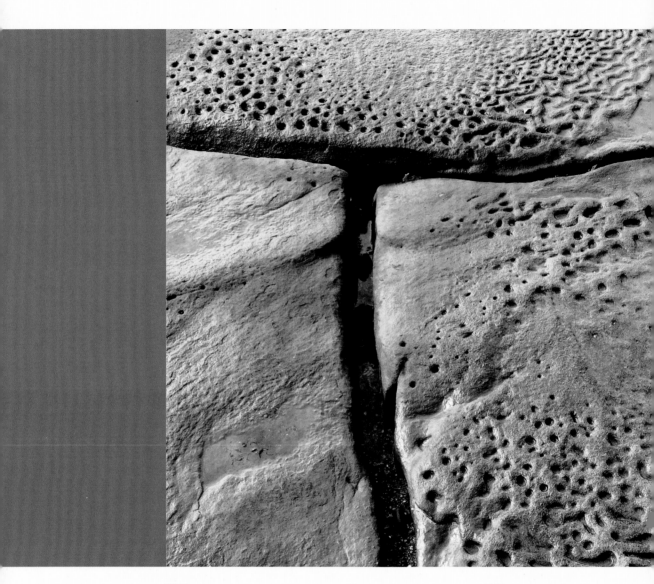

You are making it all up.

Essential Truth:

In the absence of that which you are not, that which you are, is not. That is, in the absence of cold, you cannot know the experience of warmth. In the absence of up, the idea of down is an empty, meaningless concept. This is a truth of the universe.

Yet know this: You are making it all up. You are *deciding* what is "cold" and what is "warm," what is "up" and what is "down." You are deciding what is "good" and what is "evil." And your ideas about all these things have changed through the years, even through the seasons. On a summer day you would call 42°F "cold." In the middle of winter, however, you would say, "It is a warm day!"

The universe merely provides you with a *field of experience*—what might be called a *range of objective phenomena.* You decide *what to label them.* The entire universe provides the contextual field within which all contrasting elements exist, and all experiences are thus made possible. That is the *purpose* of the universe. That is its function.

All of you have experienced *everything.* That goes for all beings in the universe, not only humans. You have all not only experienced everything, you are everything. You are ALL OF IT. You are that which you are experiencing. Indeed, you are causing the experience. You have experienced "cold." You have experienced all of it. If not in this lifetime, then in the last. Or the one before that. Or one of the many others. You have experienced "big" and "small," and "up" and "down," and "here" and "there" and every contrasting element that there is. And these are burned into your memory.

Now, here is a great secret: It is not necessary for an opposite condition to exist *right next to you* in order to provide a contextual field within which the reality that you choose may be experienced. *You do not have to experience that again if you don't want to.* You need merely remember them—know that they exist—in order to invoke the universal law of relativity.

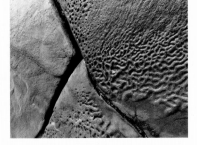

Everything revolves.

Essential Truth:

Life energy *revolves*. That is what it *does*. You are in a truly *revolutionary movement*.

What you are doing now is simply remembering everything you are, and choosing the portion of that which you prefer to experience in this moment, in this lifetime, on this planet, in this physical form.

It is *simple*. You have separated your Self from the body of God, from the All, from the Collective, and you are becoming a member of that body once again. This is the Process called "re-membering."

As you re-member, you give your Self once again all the experiences of Who You Are. This is a cycle. You do this over and over again, and call this "evolution." You say that you "evolve." Actually, you RE-volve! Just as the Earth revolves around the sun. Just as the galaxy revolves around its center.

Everything revolves. Revolution is the basic movement of all of life.

See Each Other as Who You *Really* Are.

If you choose to *be* a thing, *something or someone opposite to that has to show up somewhere in your universe* to make that possible.

Nothing you see is real.

ESSENTIAL TRUTH:

You are always seeing what by your terms you would define as the "past," even when you are looking at what is right in front of you.

It is impossible to see the Present. The Present "happens," then turns into a burst of light, formed by energy dispersing, and the light reaches your receptors, your eyes, and *it takes time for it to do that.* All the while that light is reaching you, life is *going on, moving forward.* The *next event is happening* while the light from *the last event is reaching you.*

The energy burst reaches your eyes, your receptors send that signal to your brain, which interprets the data and tells you what you are seeing. Yet that is not what is now in front of you at all. It is what you *think* you are seeing. That is, you are thinking about what you have seen, telling yourself what it is, and deciding what you are going to call it, while what is happening "now" is preceding your process, and awaiting it. The more distance you place between your Self and the physical location of an event, the further into the "past" that event recedes. Place yourself a few light-years back, and what you are looking at happened very, very long ago, indeed.

Yet it did not happen "long ago." It is merely physical distance which has created the illusion of "time," and allowed you to experience your Self as being both "here, now" all the while you are being "there, then"! One day you will see that what you call time and space are the same thing. Then you will see that everything is happening right here, right now. When you understand what I have told you, you will understand that nothing you see is real. You are seeing the image of what was once an event, yet even that image, that energy burst, is something you are interpreting. Your personal interpretation of that image is called your image-ination.

Time does not exist. It is *all happening NOW. Thus, the "past" that you re-member, and the future that you would see, is the "now" that simply IS.*

"Change" Is That Which Is.

Creative beings *can* know how they are going to feel about a thing at any time in the future, because *creative* beings create their feelings, rather than experiencing them. That which is change you are.

You *are* this. You *are* "change"—and since change is *the only thing constant about you* . . . you cannot truthfully promise to always *be the same.*

There's nothing I have to have,
there's nothing I have to do,
and there's nothing I have to be,
except exactly what I'm being right now.

ESSENTIAL TRUTH:

This does not mean that "having" and "doing" will be eliminated from your life. It means that what you experience yourself having or doing will spring *from* your being—not lead you *to it*.

When you come *from* "happiness," you do certain things because you *are* happy—as opposed to the old paradigm in which you did things that you hoped would *make* you happy.

When you come *from* "wisdom," you do certain things because you *are* wise, not because you are trying to *get* to wisdom.

When you come *from* "love," you do certain things because you *are* love, not because you want to *have* love.

Everything changes; everything turns around, when you come *from* "being," rather than seeking to "be." You cannot "do" your way to "being." Whether you are trying to "be" happy, be wise, be love—or be God—you cannot "get there" by doing. And yet, it is true that you *will* be doing wonderful things once you "get there."

Here is the Divine Dichotomy. The way to "get there" is to "be there." Just *be* where you choose to *get!* It's that simple. *There's nothing you have to do.* You want to be happy? *Be happy.* You want to be wise? *Be wise.* You want to be love? *Be love.* That is Who You Are, in any event. *You are My Beloved.*

There are three
basic wisdoms:

ESSENTIAL TRUTH:

- We Are All One—if you decided that "we are all one," you would cease treating each other the way you do.
- There's Enough—if you decided that "there's enough," you would share everything with everyone.
- There's Nothing We Have To Do—if you decided that "there's nothing we have to do," you would stop trying to use "doingness" to solve your problems, but rather would move to, and come from, a state of being which would cause your experience of those "problems" to disappear, and the conditions themselves to thus evaporate.

This is the truth I have come to share with all of you.

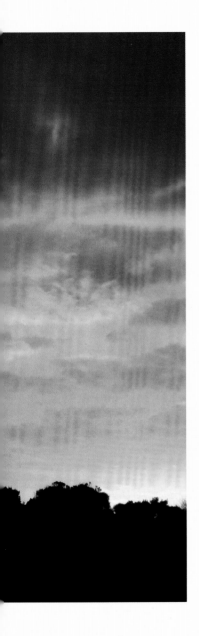

Celebrate life!
Seek to get in touch with the perfection of all things.
Know that you will be exactly where you have
to be in order to experience exactly
what you choose as you go about creating
Who You Really Are.
Celebrate! Celebrate life! Celebrate Self!
Celebrate the predictions! Celebrate God!
Bring joy to the moment, whatever the moment seems
to bring,
because joy is Who You Are, and Who You Will Always Be.
God cannot create anything imperfect.
If you think that God can create
anything imperfect, then you know nothing of God.
So celebrate. Celebrate the perfection.
Smile and celebrate and see only the perfection, and that
which others call the imperfection will not touch you in any
way which is imperfect for you.

When you DOUBT GOD you must live in fear and guilt all your life. You live your illusion, and thus feel your fear, all out of your decision to doubt God. But what if you made a new decision? What then would be the result?

I TELL YOU THIS:

You would live as the Buddha did. As Jesus did. As did every saint you have ever idolized.

When you LIVE IN FEAR you choose the energy which contracts, closes down, draws in, runs, hides, hoards, and harms.

YET I TEACH YOU THIS:

When you choose the action love sponsors, then will you do more than survive, then will you do more than win, then will you do more than succeed. Then will you experience the full glory of Who You Really Are, and who you can be.

When you JUDGE the rights
and wrongs, the do's and
don'ts, the shoulds and
shouldn'ts in God's world . . .

Remember This:

That which you condemn will condemn you,
and that which you judge, you will one day become.

If you fear RETRIBUTION
and a God Who judges and
condemns, then . . .

I Tell You This:

You are your own rule-maker. You set the guidelines. And *you* decide how well you have done; how well you are doing. For *you* are the one who has decided Who and What You Really Are—and Who You Want to Be. And *you* are the *only one* who can assess how well you're doing. No one else will judge you, ever. . . .

If you believe that life was meant to be a
STRUGGLE and that accidents happen
because they do . . .

I TELL YOU THIS:

There *is* no coincidence, and *nothing* happens "by accident." Each event and adventure is called *to* your Self *by* your Self in order that you might create and experience Who You Really Are. All true Masters know this.

The root of every problem
you experience in your life is that you
do not consider yourself worthy or deserving
enough to be SPOKEN TO BY GOD,
and yet . . .

I TELL YOU THIS:

I am performing a miracle right now. For not only am I speaking to you, but to every person who has picked up this book and is reading these words. To each of them am I now speaking. I know who every one of them is.

You must believe the
PROMISE OF GOD that you
are His son, Her offspring, Its
likeness, His equal. For . . .

I TELL YOU THIS:

All you see in *your world is the outcome of your idea about it.* For if you are God's *equal,* that means nothing is being done *to* you—and all things are created *by* you. *There can be no more victims and no more villains*—only outcomes of your thought about a thing.

Can you believe that the WORD
OF GOD is not a commandment,
but a divine covenant?

YET I TELL YOU THIS:

I am neither a king nor a ruler. I am simply—and awesomely—the Creator. Yet the Creator does not rule, but merely creates, creates—and keeps on creating. I have created you—blessed you—in the image and likeness of Me. And I have made certain promises and commitments to you.

Do you imagine that
you can EXPERIENCE
something that
God cannot?

I TELL YOU THIS:

Every experience you have, I have. Do you not see I am
experiencing my Self *through* you? What else do you sup-
pose all this is for? I could not know Myself were it not for
You. I *created* you that I might know Who I Am.

The POINT OF
LIFE is not to
get anywhere—it
is to notice that
you are, and have
always been,
already there.

YET KNOW THIS:

There is no such thing as an incorrect path—for on this journey you cannot "not get" where you are going. *The point of life is therefore to create Who and What You Are, and then to experience that.*

If God has no judgment one way
or the other as to how I live my
life—how do I know the TRUTH
of what is "right" from "wrong"?

I'll Tell You This,
To Help You Out
Of Your Dilemma:

Believe *nothing* I say. Simply *live it*. Experience it. Then live whatever other paradigm you want to construct. Afterward, look to your *experience* to find your truth.

It's when the going gets tough and we forget Who We Are

that we need more than ever to go to our GOD SPACE.

For it is from there that we can see things in their proper

perspective and use the tools we have been given.

YET I TELL YOU THIS:

When you follow Me, the struggle disappears.

Live in your God space and the events

become blessings, one and all.

If you aren't happy with the things in life that you've CREATED, that you have called forth, then choose, choose again. For . . .

I Tell You This:

You *always* get what you create,

and you are *always* creating.

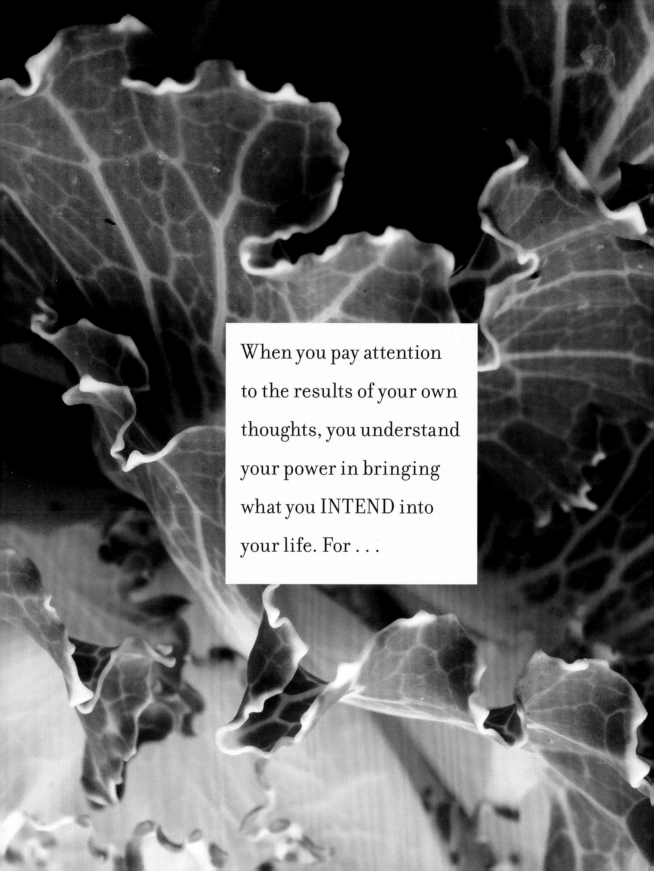

When you pay attention
to the results of your own
thoughts, you understand
your power in bringing
what you INTEND into
your life. For . . .

I Tell You This:

Your Life proceeds out of your

intentions *for it.*

For a relationship to work, you need to be SELF-CENTERED. Worry only about what you are being. For if you cannot love yourself you cannot love another.

AND SO I TELL YOU THIS:

Be now and forever centered upon your Self. Look to see what you are being, doing, and having in any given moment, *not* what's going on with another.

In your RELATIONSHIP with another,
are you creating the experience of your
highest conceptualization of *self*, or your
highest conceptualization of the *other*?

YET I TELL YOU THIS:

Your focus upon the other—your *obsession* with the other—is what causes relationships to fail.

When you approach life from the vantage point that "I am my soul," your life will unfold in only love-sponsored actions. For you are *not* fear, you are LOVE.

FOR I TELL YOU THIS:

At the critical juncture in all human relationships, there is only one question: *What would love do now?*

You may think that love-sponsored action arises out of the choice to be, do, and have whatever produces the HIGHEST GOOD for *another*!

YET I TELL YOU THIS:

The highest choice is that
which produces the highest good *for you*.

Do you include yourself among those you LOVE? Do you put yourself first? Does it seem that the act of choosing what is "best" for *you* in your life causes hurt to another?

I TELL YOU THIS:

Putting yourself first in the highest sense *never* leads to an ungodly act. If, therefore, you have caught yourself in an ungodly act as a result of doing what is best for you, the confusion is not in having put yourself first, but rather in misunderstanding what is best for you.

What state of BEINGNESS are you selecting as you encounter life? Are you choosing what you really *desire* for yourself, from the enormous menu of experiences available?

I TELL YOU THIS:

Beingness attracts beingness,

and produces experience.

Do you grasp that your magnificent BODY was designed to last forever—created as a divine tool, a vehicle, through which you may know the Self you have created in your soul?

I Tell You This:

You were not meant

to ever die.

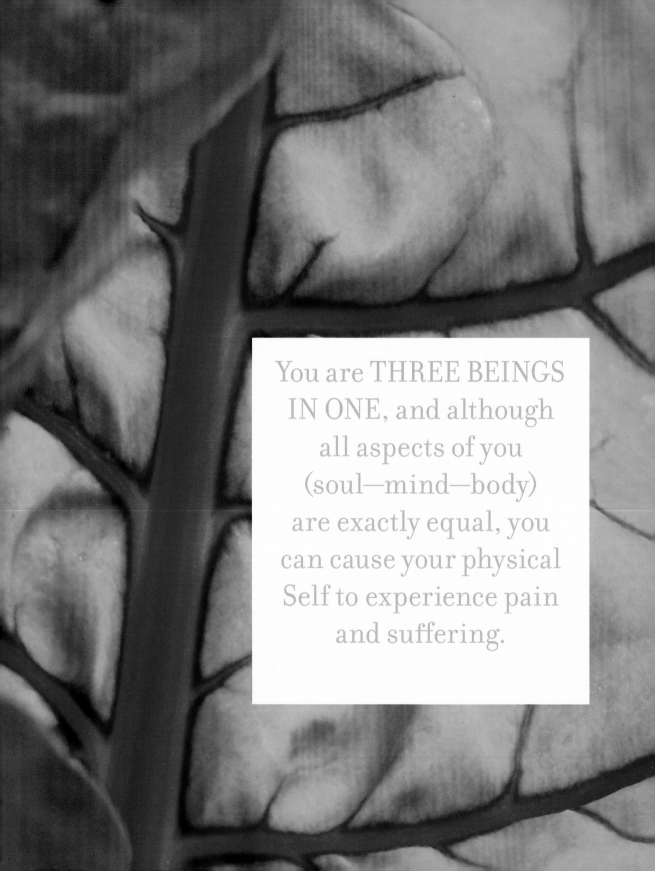

You are THREE BEINGS IN ONE, and although all aspects of you (soul—mind—body) are exactly equal, you can cause your physical Self to experience pain and suffering.

YET THIS MUCH
IS SO:

The soul will never

override the body

or the mind.

Do you comprehend WHO YOU ARE?
Can you believe all of it (including you) *is*
God, and there is nothing else?

I TELL YOU THIS:

I AM THAT I AM. And YOU ARE THAT YOU ARE. *You cannot not be.* You can change form all you wish, but you cannot fail to be. Yet you *can* fail to *know* Who You Are—and in this failing, *experience only the half of it.*

You have been given this life. Do you realize there is no limit to what you can BECOME?

FOR I TELL YOU THIS:

You are *already* a God. *You simply do not know it.* Have I not said, "Ye are Gods"?

Do you want guarantees ahead of time
that all your choices will be "good"? Then
you will need to be OUT OF YOUR MIND
and in the *pre-sent* moment when you
choose. So . . .

REMEMBER THIS:

The soul creates, the mind reacts.

It can prove hard to honor your FEELINGS, because we have labeled growth as "trouble" and standing still as "safe." But you must not filter every feeling through the machinery of the mind, because . . .

I Tell You This:

Your feelings will *never* get you into
"trouble," because your feelings
are your *truth*.

Are you afraid to express your TRUTH for fear of the unpleasantness it may cause? Then *always* express your truth with love.

REMEMBER THIS:

*It is not nearly so important how well
a message is received as how well it is sent.*

Your FEELINGS are real, not "made-up" creations of your mind. So get out of your mind and get back to your senses to know what is best for you.

Remember This:

True celebration

is mindless.

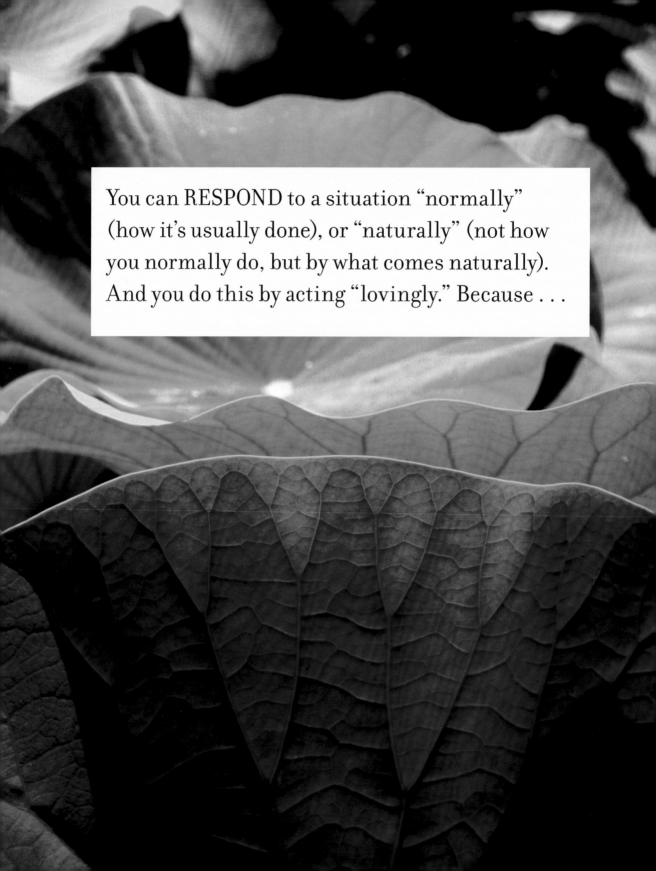

You can RESPOND to a situation "normally" (how it's usually done), or "naturally" (not how you normally do, but by what comes naturally). And you do this by acting "lovingly." Because . . .

I TELL YOU THIS:

Nothing is more
natural than love.

Do you know what you are doing here, why you have come to this world in this way, at this time, in this place? You are a Being of magnificent possibility and you are here not only to Know Who You Are, but to create WHO YOU WISH to BE.

I Tell You This:

Men have achieved results much greater than flying.

Men have healed sickness.

Men have raised the dead.

When you consciously seek, choose,
and demonstrate that you are ONE
WITH GOD, whatever you call forth will
manifest in your reality.

I TELL YOU
THIS . . . AGAIN:

Seek and ye shall find.

Knock and it shall be

opened to you.

If you truly seek UNITY with God like Jesus and Moses, then you need to be constantly on the path and *"walk your talk"* as they did. For . . .

I Tell You This:

You want to be "Christed"? *Act* like Christ, *every minute of every day*. He has left you with *instructions*. You are not without help in this, should you seek it.

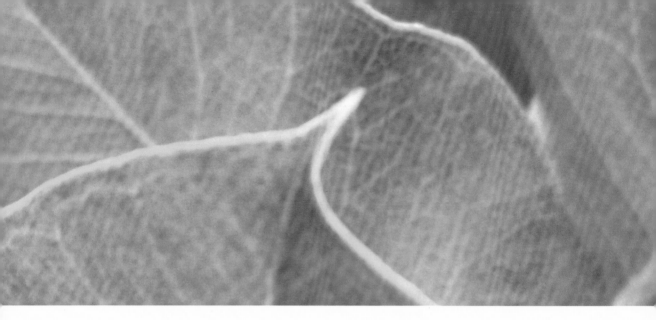

Have you ever had the REALIZATION that you've done this before? That it is right *now* that everything is happening? Have you felt that . . . *forever is a right now thing?*

I TELL YOU THIS:

You have always been, are now, and always will be. There has *never* been a time when you were not—nor will there ever *be* such a time.

There is no human being less perfect than another. There are only those who have defined different RULES and BOUNDARIES for their actions. That is why . . .

I TELL YOU THIS:

There *is* no evil.

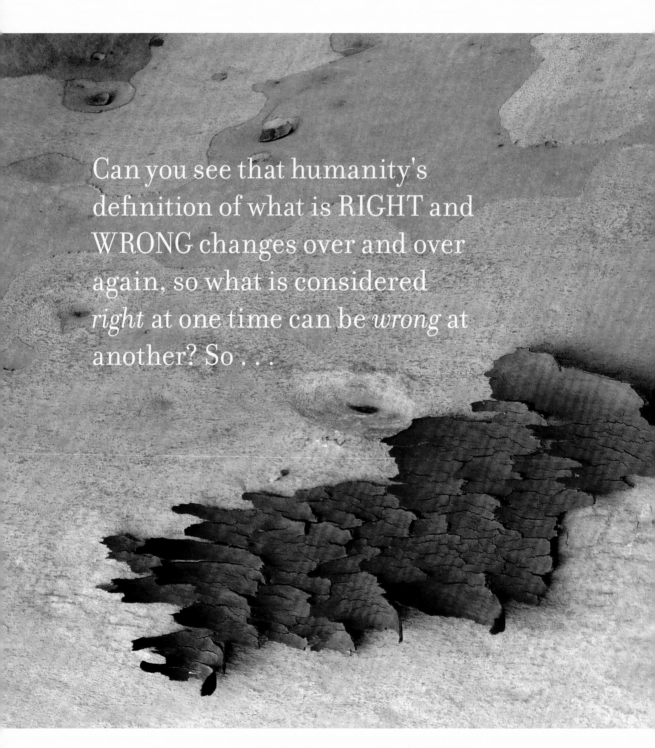

Can you see that humanity's definition of what is RIGHT and WRONG changes over and over again, so what is considered *right* at one time can be *wrong* at another? So . . .

I Am Going to Tell You This:

There are *no* "rotten apples." There are only people who *disagree with your point of view on things*, people who construct a different model of the world. I am going to tell you this: no one does anything inappropriate, given their model of the world.

In our realm of relativity, GOOD cannot
exist without *bad*. So do you believe it
must be the same in God's realm?

I Tell You This:

There *is* no "bad" where I Am. And there is no evil. There is only the All of Everything. The Oneness. And the awareness, the Experience, of that. Mine is the Realm of the Absolute, where One Thing does not exist in relationship to Another, but quite independent of anything. Mine is the place where All There Is is love.

If you can accept the truth of what we call DEATH, you come to the realization that it is the greatest thing that would happen to anyone. For . . .

I TELL YOU THIS:

At the moment of your death, you will realize the greatest freedom, the greatest peace, the greatest joy, and the greatest love you have ever known.

Do you know
what the purpose
of your life is, and
what it is that GOD
WANTS of you?

I Tell You This:

The purpose of life is not to please God. The purpose of life is to know, and to re-create, Who You Are. In so doing, you *do* please God, and glorify *Her* as well.

When you want the world to
CHANGE, change the things
in your own world and thus
shift the consciousness of
others *by your example.*

The Thing to Remember Is:

Consciousness is everything, and creates your experience. *Group* consciousness is powerful and produces outcomes of unspeakable beauty or ugliness. The choice is always yours.

Would you condemn or bless the actions of ADAM and EVE?

I TELL YOU THIS:

They were said to have committed Original Sin. It was the Original Blessing. For without this event, the partaking of the knowledge of good and evil, *you* would not even know the two possibilities existed! Indeed, before the so-called Fall of Adam, these two possibilities *did not* exist. There *was* no "evil." Everyone and everything existed in a state of constant perfection. It was, literally, paradise. Yet you didn't *know* it was paradise—could not experience it as perfection—because you knew *nothing else.*

Rejoice in the wonder that you are a DIVINE BEING, much larger than you think, and you exist everywhere—and at all times!

JUST KNOW THIS:

You are a being of Divine Proportion,
knowing no limitation. A part of you
is choosing to know yourself as your
presently experienced identity. Yet this
is by far not the limit of your Being,
although you *think that it is.*

When reflecting on crime, it is necessary for man to understand that no one does anything that is WRONG given their model of the world.

I TELL YOU THIS:

God's love and God's compassion, God's wisdom and God's forgiveness, God's intention and God's *purpose,* are large enough to include the most heinous crime and the most heinous criminal.

Go ahead and CHOOSE the adulation of others, being better, having more, knowing how and why. But choose to know God *first*, and all else will follow.

I TELL YOU THIS:

Love, love, *love* the things you desire—for your love of them *draws them to you. These things are the stuff of life.* When you love them, you love *life!*

Do you know WHO YOU ARE? Then give yourself the pleasure of the experience of *feeling good* . . . often. For that is the road to heaven! "Feeling good" is the soul's way of shouting, "This is who I am!"

I Tell You This:

No kind of evolution ever took place through *denial*. If you are to evolve, it will not be because you've been able to successfully *deny* yourself the things that you *know* "feel good," but because you've *granted* yourself these pleasures—and found something even greater. For how can you know that something is "greater" if you've never tasted the "lesser"?

Genuine appreciation
for *all* of life is what honors
the PROCESS God has
created. So do not call
any creation unholy.
For . . .

I TELL YOU THIS:

I have created *nothing* disdainful—
and, as your Shakespeare said,
nothing is "evil" lest thinking
make it so.

Always be sensitive, keenly aware, and err
on the side of *love* when you tell your loved
one your TRUTH, and yet always be true
to your own Self.

I TELL YOU THIS:

Man *is* capable of making the *highest* choice. Yet I also tell you this: the Highest Choice is not *always* the choice which seems to serve another.

If you do not include LOVE in what you are preparing or consuming, you're missing the most extraordinary part of the experience.

Let Me Just Say This:

Loveless *anything* is not
the fastest way to the Goddess.

When you teach your children "knowledge," you teach *what* to think instead of *how* to think. When you give WISDOM, you show the child how to get to their own truth. So let the child make his or her own discoveries.

Know This:

Knowledge is lost.

Wisdom is never forgotten.

Until you *also* take RESPONSIBILITY
for the choices made by mankind,
the same mistakes will be repeated.

I TELL YOU THIS:

Until you are willing to take responsibility for all of it, *you cannot change any of it*. You keep saying *they* did it, and *they* are doing it, and if only they would get it right! Remember the wonderful line from Walt Kelly's comic strip character, Pogo, and never forget it: *"We have met the enemy, and they is us."*

If you could move deep within the soul
to GOD CONSCIOUSNESS while in
the midst of a tragedy, you would
be able to see the glory of
the process.

THIS IS DIFFICULT TO HEAR, BUT I TELL YOU THIS:

There is perfection in everything.

Strive to see the perfection.

When you err on the side of
COMPASSION for your fellow man,
the result is an outpouring
of basic human dignity.

I Tell You This:

Compassion never ends, love never stops, patience never runs out in God's World. Only in the world of man is goodness limited. *In My World, goodness is endless.*

When you are being ATTACKED, try to see the deeper picture. All people are doing the best they can at any given moment. No one truly desires to hurt another. Because . . .

I HAVE TOLD
YOU BEFORE:

All attack is a call for help.

Remember that you are the GIFT.
When someone enters your life
unexpectedly, *look for the gift
that person has come to
receive from you.*

I Tell You This:

Every person who has ever come to you has come to receive a gift from you. In so doing, he gives a gift to you—the gift of your experiencing and fulfilling Who You Are.

In a SOCIETY where nothing is hidden, no one is willing to get anything or have anything at someone else's expense. The chief aim is providing a good life for *all*.

I Tell You This:

Nothing breeds fairness faster
than visibility. *Visibility* is simply
another word for *truth*.

When you have found God, and when you have found your TRUTH, it is not necessary to talk about it. It is self-evident.

YET I TELL YOU THIS:

Truth and God are found in the same place:

in the silence.

The Eternal Moment of Now is *forever changing*—
it is always there, but constantly shifting.
So, too, YOU are deciding and changing your
reality *now*.

I TELL YOU THIS:

Your future is creatable.

Create it as you want.

It is RELIGION that has separated man
from God, man from man, man from woman.
Return to spirituality and forget religion.
Go back to the source within.

I TELL YOU THIS:

God is *not* above man, and man is *not* above woman—that is *not* the "natural order of things"—but it *is* the way everyone who had power (namely men) *wished* it was when they formed their male-worshipping religions, systematically editing out half the material from their final version of the "holy scriptures" and twisting the rest to fit the mold of their male model of the world.

There is no one person or class of people more "suited" to teach the Word of God, preach the Word of God, or do MY WORK than any other.

I Tell You This:

You are *all* priests. *Every single one of you.*

Many men are like nations—they do not like to *share* their POWER. And nations merely exercise their power. They have thus constructed a power-hungry God.

YET I TELL YOU THIS:

God's greatest gift is the sharing of God's power. I *would have you be like Me.*

It is time to BELIEVE in the goodness of God's creation—namely, your holy Self. For . . .

I Tell You This:

You have been made in the Image and Likeness of God—it is the destiny you came to fulfill. You did not come here to strive and to struggle and to never "get there." Nor did I send you on a mission impossible to complete.

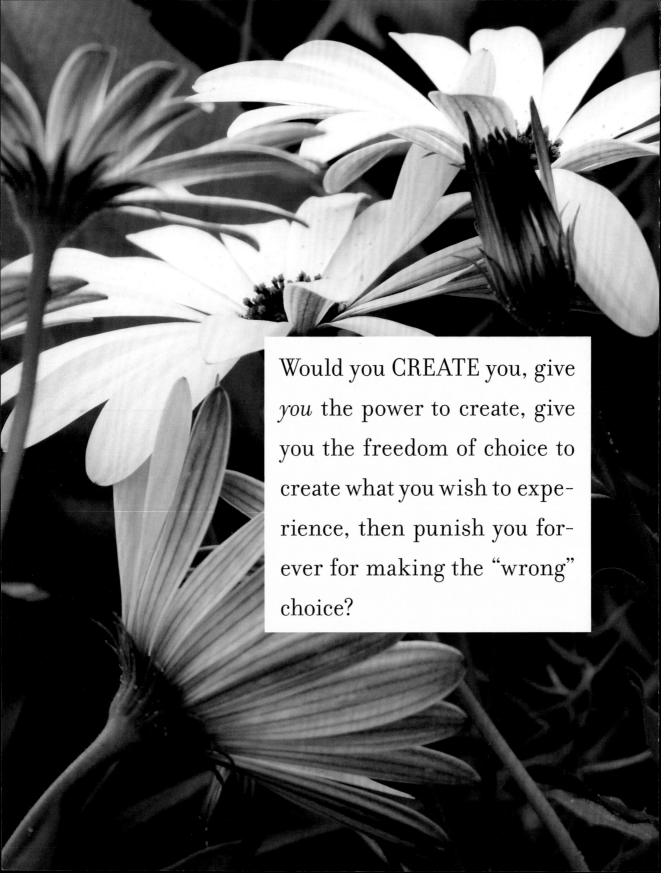

Would you CREATE you, give *you* the power to create, give you the freedom of choice to create what you wish to experience, then punish you forever for making the "wrong" choice?

I Tell You This:

I would not do such a thing—and in that truth lies your freedom from the tyranny of God. In truth, there *is* no tyranny—except in your imagination.

Do you require APPROVAL

from outside yourself?

Yet I Tell You This:

So long as you are still worried about what others think of you, you are owned by them. Only when you require no approval from outside yourself can you own yourself.

Do you sometimes feel GUILTY? Then remember that guilt is the feeling that keeps you stuck in who you are *not*!

I TELL YOU THIS:

Guilt is a blight upon the land—the poison that kills the plant. You will not grow through guilt, but only shrivel and die.

What MESSAGES do you send
out to others? Seek only to be
genuine. Strive to be
sincere.

Remember This Also:

You teach what you have to learn.

When you get stuck in your FEAR, block yourself, sabotage yourself from moving ahead, remember God's promise . . .

I TELL YOU THIS:

There is never a time when I am not with you; never a moment when I am not "ready." Yet I will not impose My will on you—ever.

Life is not about POWER, but about strength. Not about separation, but unity. For in the unity *inner strength exists*, in separation it dissipates, leaving you powerless—struggling for power.

I Tell You This:

Heal the rift between you, end the illusion of separation, and you shall be delivered back to the source of your inner strength. That is where you will find true power. The power to do anything. The power to be anything. The power to have anything. For the power to create is derived from the inner strength that is produced through unity.

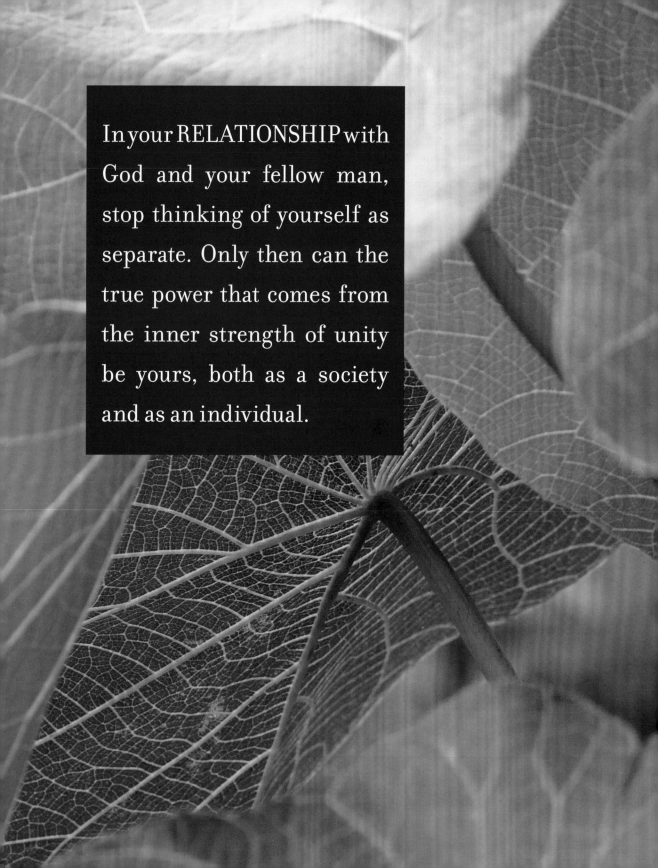

In your RELATIONSHIP with God and your fellow man, stop thinking of yourself as separate. Only then can the true power that comes from the inner strength of unity be yours, both as a society and as an individual.

YET REMEMBER THIS:

Power comes from inner strength. Inner strength does not come from raw power. In this, most of the world has it backward. Power without inner strength is an illusion. Inner strength without unity is a lie.

Act as if you are SEPARATE
from nothing, and you heal the world.
For it is about power *with*, not
power *over*.

Now I Tell You This:

Know the truth, and the truth shall set you free. There is no separation. Not from each other, not from God, and not from anything that is.

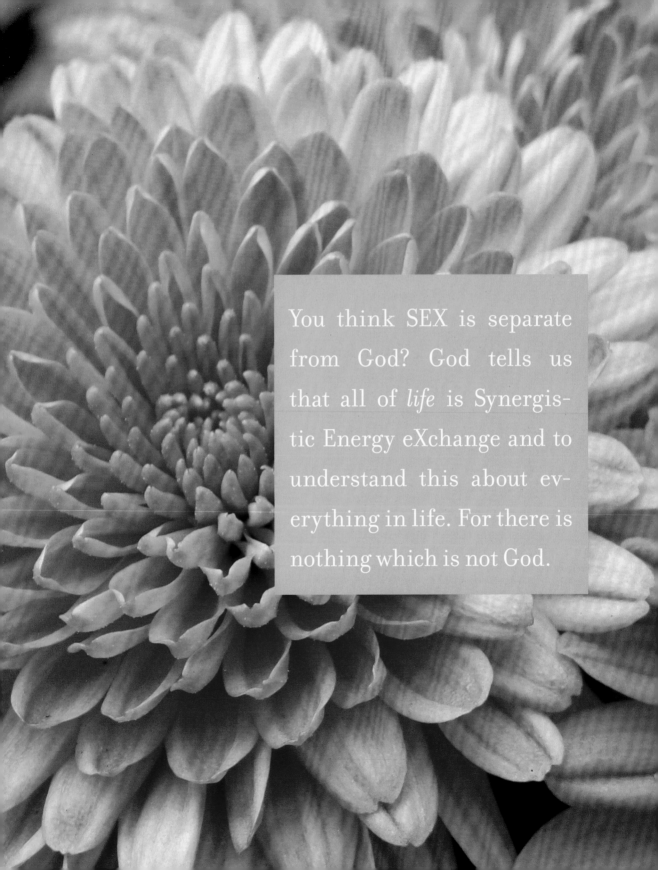

You think SEX is separate from God? God tells us that all of *life* is Synergistic Energy eXchange and to understand this about everything in life. For there is nothing which is not God.

I TELL YOU THIS:

I am in your bedroom every night.

Consider the Parable of
the Rock. This explains
the Cosmology that
LIFE is moving
(the particle) and not
moving (the rock)
at the *same time*.

AND I TELL YOU THIS:

Upon this Rock, I will build My Church. For this is the Rock of Ages. This is the eternal truth that leaves no stone unturned. I have explained it all for you here, in this little story. This is the Cosmology.

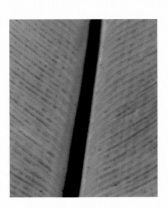

Do you allow the COLLECTIVE consciousness to create "the moment" in
your reality? Be aware of the importance of the company you keep.

I Would Tell You This:

It is when you are surrounded by lower consciousness that you will benefit more from remaining with your individual understanding, and when you are surrounded by higher consciousness that you receive greater benefit from surrender.

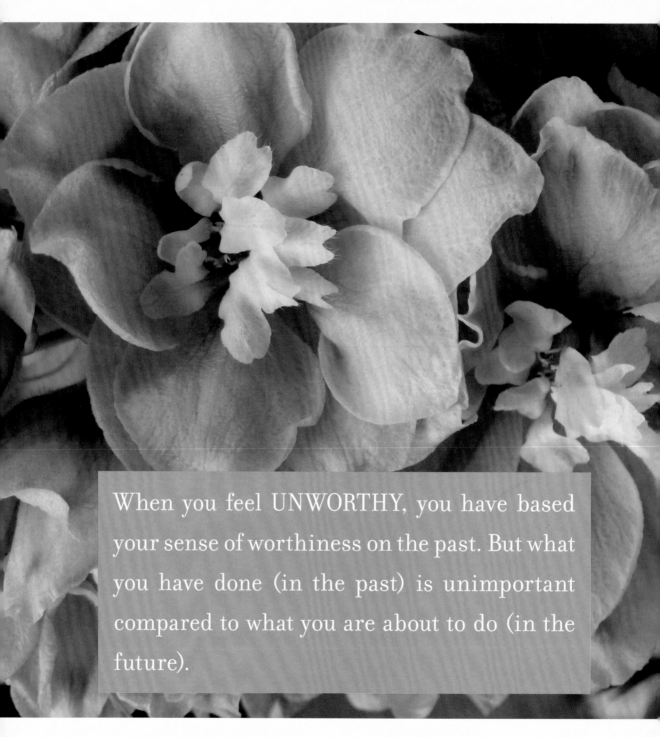

When you feel UNWORTHY, you have based your sense of worthiness on the past. But what you have done (in the past) is unimportant compared to what you are about to do (in the future).

YET I TELL YOU THIS:

You *are* worthy. As is everyone else. Unworthiness is the worst indictment ever visited upon the human race.

It's a very rare SOUL who desires to return to physicality in the same form as before. It almost always does so with another body; a different one. And yet . . .

I TELL YOU THIS:

Many have there been who have been risen from the "dead." Many have there been who have "come back to life." It's happening every day, right now, in your hospitals.

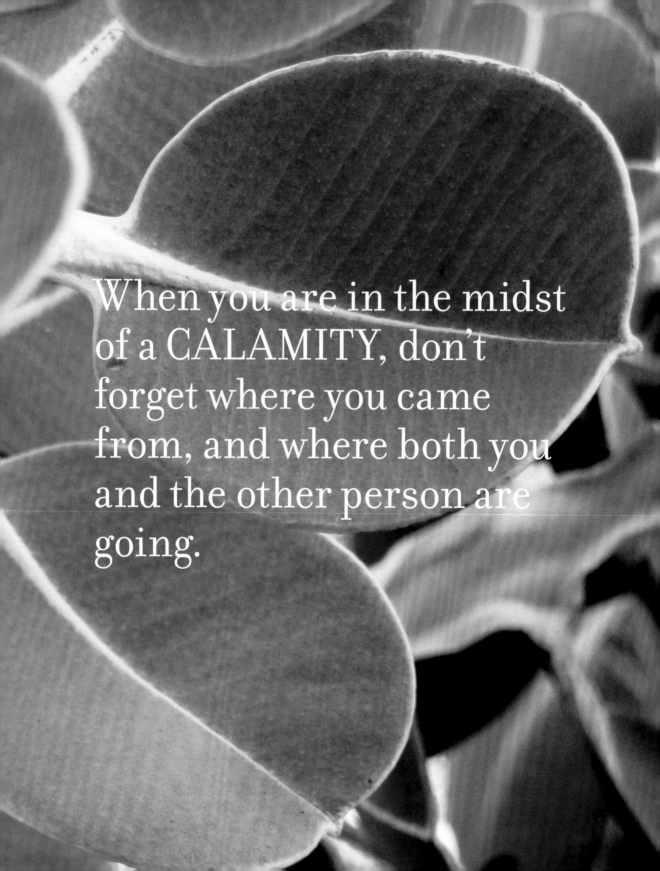

When you are in the midst of a CALAMITY, don't forget where you came from, and where both you and the other person are going.

I TELL YOU THIS:

There is not a one among you who is lost forever, nor will there ever be. For you are all, *all*, in the process of becoming. You are all, *all*, moving through the experience of evolution. That is what I am up to. Through you.

That which you wish for yourself, give to another. Because you and the other are ONE and so what you give to another, you give to *yourself.*

AND I WILL TELL YOU THIS:

The day will come when
we will speak as One. That day will
come for all people.

Do you believe that things
"just happen," "just appear" at
"just the right moment"
by CHANCE?

I Tell You This:

There are no coincidences in the universe.

SUICIDE is merely a question of "timing." The faster the death, the more "wrong" it seems to be.

Now I Tell You This:

It is no more immoral to kill yourself quickly than it is to kill yourself slowly.

When you raise the energy of life through your physical being (the chakras), the more ELEVATED will be your consciousness.

So Now I Tell You This:

The more elevated a society or being, the more elevated are its pleasures. What you call "pleasure" is what declares your level of evolution.

We are all the same energy, coalesced, compressed in different ways to create different forms and different matter. And so the Great Mystery is that there is only ONE OF US, and it is That Which You Are!

I TELL YOU THIS:

We are all the *same stuff*.

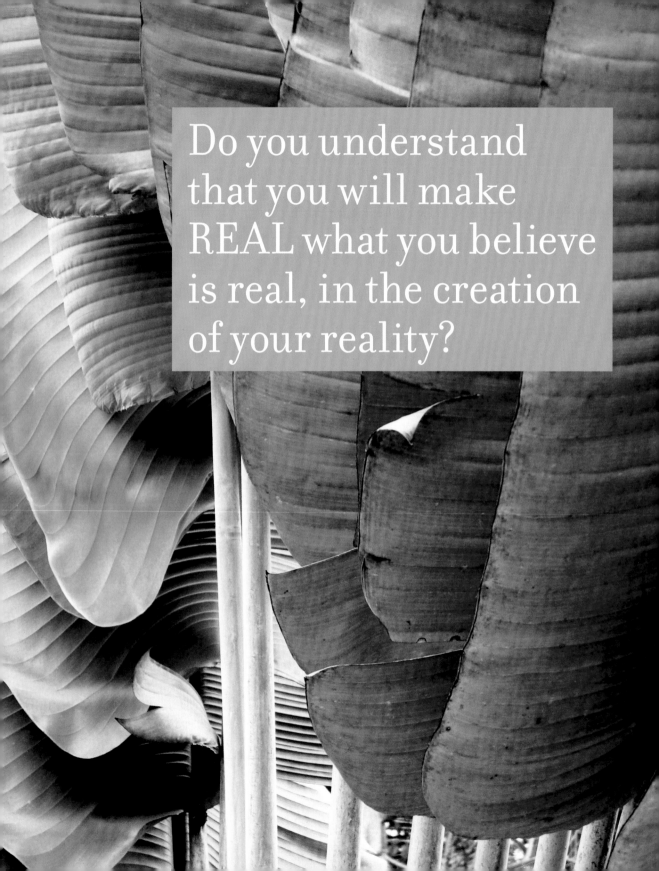

Do you understand that you will make REAL what you believe is real, in the creation of your reality?

YET I TELL YOU THIS:

Your life was never meant to be a struggle, and doesn't have to be, now or ever. I have given you the tools with which to create the grandest reality.

When special PROMISES are made, it may come to pass that they will be experienced as an *obligation* and be resented. Therefore do not make one promise for forever, but make free choice over and over again, always from within a space of love.

Remember This:

There is only one sacred promise—and that is to *tell and live your truth*. All other promises are forfeitures of freedom, and that can never be sacred.

In human terms,
there appears
to be great
constancy in
our universe.
However, life is
really a process of
RE-CREATION—
re-creating itself
anew in each
moment of now.

Yet I Tell You This:

Viewed from the perspective of all life (that which is physical and that which is nonphysical), the appearance of constancy disappears. Things are experienced as they *really are:* constantly changing.

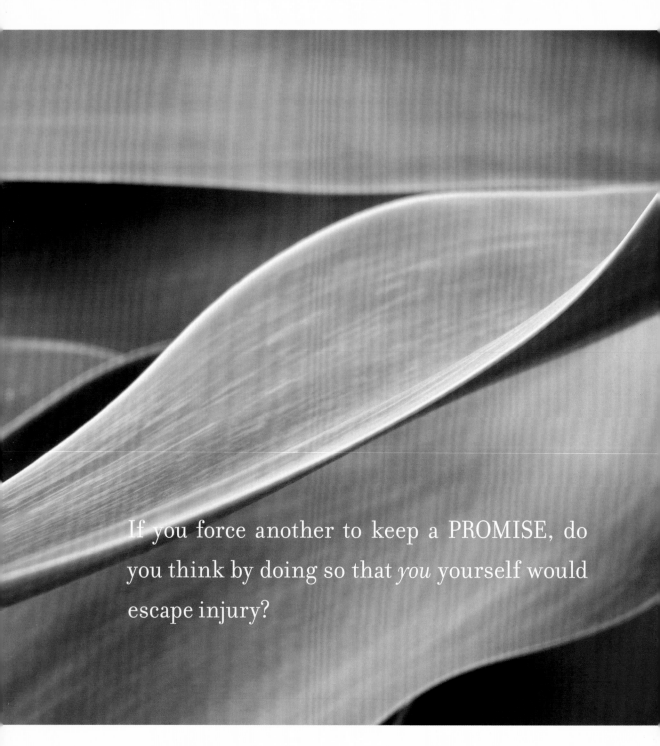

If you force another to keep a PROMISE, do you think by doing so that *you* yourself would escape injury?

I TELL YOU THIS:

More damage has been done to others by persons leading lives of quiet desperation (that is, doing what they felt they "had" to do) than ever was done by persons freely doing what they wanted to do.

Man has constructed the institutions of both religion and marriage, as proof that God loves one
group of people more than another. But God's culture is based on INCLUSION, not exclusion.

I Tell You This:

You have bastardized the Word of God in order to justify your fears and rationalize your insane treatment of each other.

The one TRUTH we cannot accept is that in God's love, *everyone* is included, in God's kingdom—*everyone* is invited.

I TELL YOU THIS:

My love is unlimited and unconditional. That is the one thing you cannot hear, the one truth you cannot abide, the one statement you cannot accept, for its all-inclusiveness destroys not only the institution of marriage (as you have constructed it), but every one of your religious and governmental institutions as well.

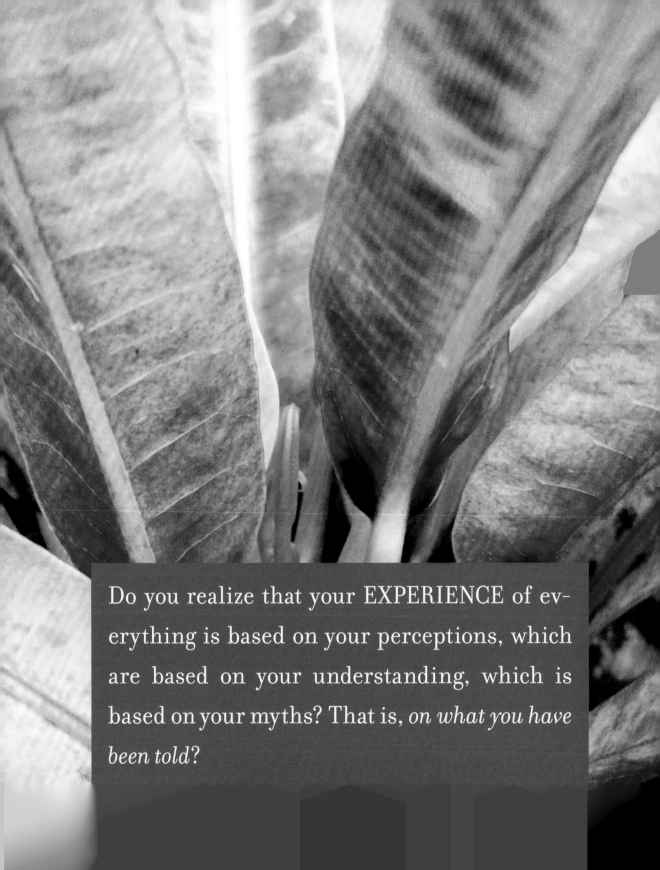

Do you realize that your EXPERIENCE of everything is based on your perceptions, which are based on your understanding, which is based on your myths? That is, *on what you have been told?*

Now I Tell You This:

Your present cultural myths have not served you. They have not taken you where you say you want to go. Either you are lying to yourself about where you say you want to go, or you are blind to the fact that you are not getting there. Not as an individual, not as a country, not as a species or a race.

Do you think your earthly REALITY, right here, right now on this planet, *is all that's going on?*

I Tell You This:

You are "in this world, but not of it."

We have constructed *complete theologies* and *entire lives* on a kind of tortured logic that we are SEPARATE from God and each other. However, everything we are doing is in concert *with* each other.

I TELL YOU THIS:

The time has come for you to look at things a new way. This is the moment of your rebirth, as an individual and as a society. You must re-create your world now, before you destroy it with your insanities. Now *listen to Me*. We are All One. There is only One of Us.

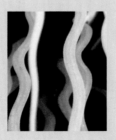

When you are DECIDING all things (whether the choice is major or minor), there is only one question to consider: Is this Who I Really Am? Is this who I now choose to be? For you are in the act of defining your Self right now.

AND UNDERSTAND THIS:

No matter is inconsequential. There is a consequence to
everything. The consequence is who and what you are.

Until you "see" the master plan and your part in the cycle of illusion, the game of life will go on. Indeed it must, and in the meantime . . . you will DENY What You Really Are.

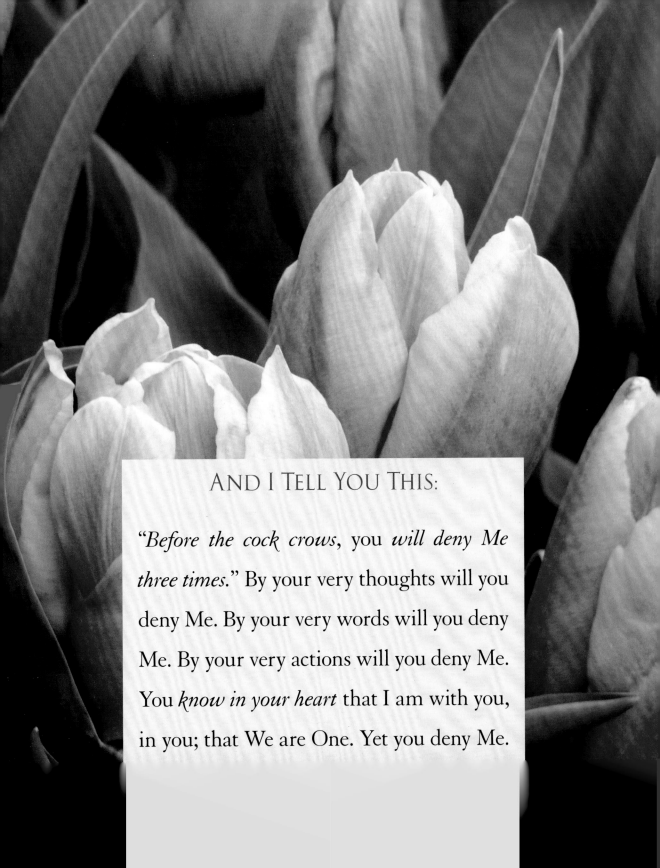

AND I TELL YOU THIS:

"*Before the cock crows*, you *will deny Me three times.*" By your very thoughts will you deny Me. By your very words will you deny Me. By your very actions will you deny Me. You *know in your heart* that I am with you, in you; that We are One. Yet you deny Me.

Do you believe that
God CREATED
you?

I Come Now to Tell You This:

You are creating God. That is a massive rearrangement of your understanding, I know. And yet it is a necessary one if you are to go about the true work for which you came.

You, the You who is reading these words, have come to this material for a reason, and it is part of the "master plan." *The plan for how you become a MASTER.*

I TELL YOU THIS:

I know every person who will come to this material. And I know the reason each has been brought. And so do they. Now the only question is, will they deny Me again?

An advanced society is at the level of knowingness that you and the other are ONE. But when you have advanced technology without advanced thought, it creates not advancement, but demise.

I TELL YOU THIS:

You cannot have advanced technologies in any beneficial way without advanced thinking.

To say our CULTURE is "primitive" is not a judgment, but
merely a description of what
is so, what is true. It says that
we are in the very early stages
of development, nothing more
than that. It does not mean our
culture is "right" or "wrong."

Understand This:

An assessment is not a judgment. It is merely an observation of What Is.

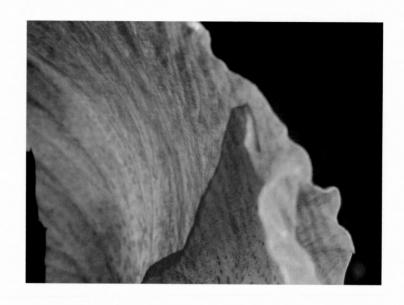

In spite of all our primitive QUALITIES, God looks at us and sees only beauty and wonder. For our grandest ideas are as yet unexpressed, and our grandest vision unlived.

AND I TELL YOU THIS:

The beauty and the fragrance of your flowering shall fill the land, and you shall yet have your place in the Garden of the Gods.

God does not impose some form

of celestial justice in

the AFTERLIFE.

I TELL YOU THIS:

There *is* no "afterlife," but *only* life. Death does not exist.
And the way you experience and create your life, as individuals and as a society, is your demonstration of what you
think is just.

It is not heaven's role to correct what you call "injustice." Therefore, do not seek JUSTICE after an injustice, but rather by "doing justice" in the first place.

AND I TELL YOU THIS:

The rain falls on the just and
the unjust alike.

Highly evolved beings do not see SCARCITY of a product as an opportunity for greater profits, nor do they see the need for communicating the meaning of "yours" and "mine." In these cultures it is not possible to fail to share.

YET I TELL YOU THIS:

Until your *community of beings* knows about *being in community,* you will never experience Holy Communion, and cannot know Who I Am.

Remember always that God is a work in progress, and so are you. You are a human, comma, BEING, and you are *magnificent*!

And Remember This Always:

If you saw you as God sees you, you would smile a lot.

Have you sometimes been APART FROM GOD in your heart? Then listen to this—you are Truth, you are Joy, and you are Love. You are these three interchangeable things and one leads to the other. All of them *lead* to God. All of them *are* God, too, just like you! So . . .

Remember This:

You are always a part, because you are never apart. You are always a part OF God, because you are never apart FROM God. This is the truth of your being. We are whole. So now you know the whole truth.

In Closing

"I Will Not Leave You"

"There's a lot here to absorb. A lot to wrestle with. A lot to ponder. Take some time off. Reflect on this. Ponder it. Do not feel abandoned. I am always with you. If you have questions—day-to-day questions—as I know you do even now, and will continue to—know that you can call on Me to answer them. You do not need the form of this book.

"This is not the only way I speak to you. Listen to Me in the truth of your soul. Listen to Me in the feelings of your heart. Listen to Me in the quiet of your mind. Hear Me, everywhere. Whenever you have a question, simply *know* that I have answered it *already*. Then open your eyes to your world. My response could be in an article already published. In the sermon already written and about to be delivered. In the movie now being made. In the song just yesterday composed. In the words about to be said by a loved one. In the heart of a new friend about to be made. My truth is in the whisper of the wind, the babble of the brook, the crack of the thunder, the tap of the rain. It is the feel of the earth, the fragrance of the lily, the warmth of the sun, the pull of the moon. My truth—and your surest help in time of need—is as awesome as the night sky, and as simply, incontrovertibly trustful as a baby's gurgle. It is as loud as a pounding heartbeat—and as quiet as a breath taken in unity with Me.

"I will not leave you, I *cannot* leave you, for you are My creation and My product, My daughter and My son, My purpose and My . . . Self. Call on Me, therefore, wherever and whenever you are separate from the peace that I am. I will be there. With Truth. And Light. And Love."

ABOUT THE AUTHORS

Neale Donald Walsch (author) has written thirty-three books on contemporary spirituality and its practical application in everyday life. Seven of the nine books in his *Conversations with God* series have made the *New York Times* bestseller list, with Book One remaining on that list for 134 weeks. His titles have been translated into thirty-seven languages and have sold millions around the world. He is the founder of CWG Connect (www.CWGConnect.com), a global online platform connecting people around the world who wish to explore more deeply the insights in the CWG cosmology, and the creator of the School of the New Spirituality and its home schooling program (www.cwgforparents.com).

Sherr Robertson (coauthor and photographer) has been a spoiled wife for over forty years, a lucky mom of two great kids, and is now a blessed "Nan" of five scrumptious grandsons. She lives in the beautiful state of Queensland, Australia. She says her life was deeply touched and changed for the better forever by the messages in the *Conversations with God* books, and that this moved her to produce brief written expansions of what they meant for her, then to send those writings, along with her personally-taken photographs, to Neale Donald Walsch as a gift. The combination of those contributions and the CWG material in one book has created this coauthored project.